THE MINISTER LOOKS AT HIMSELF

By the Same Author

THE MEANING OF CHURCH MEMBERSHIP

The MINISTER
LOOKS AT HIMSELF

By *WAYNE C. CLARK*

In this book an authority on religion and mental
health addresses his fellow-ministers and offers
them friendly counsel with respect to their most
difficult problems—those arising within their own
personalities.

PHILADELPHIA

THE JUDSON PRESS

CHICAGO   LOS ANGELES

PRINTED IN THE U.S.A.

CONTENTS

Continued on next page

5

The minister is not exempt from sin and guilt; sometimes his distress is due to overconscientiousness; in the latter case he needs a right attitude toward our human limitations; where there has been actual sin, he must make confession and ask the divine forgiveness.

6

The minister, sometimes without realizing it, may assume an attitude of superiority; this attitude often designated the God-complex; the ways in which this attitude finds expression; how the minister may overcome his conceit.

7

The minister must accept reality; this calls for a personal adjustment to life; it calls equally for a personal adjustment to death; the hope which inspires the Christian to a dedicated life.

FOREWORD

THE MINISTER'S MOST FORMIDABLE ANTAGONISTS may not be in the outer world, but within himself. Indeed, it is wholly possible that his external conflicts will lessen in intensity, even disappear, if he will face his inner conflicts and come to understand them. This is true because our world really is more subjective than it is objective. We interpret it with our feelings. We read into it our emotions. If our emotional state is tranquil, so will be our world; if our emotional state is disturbed, so will be our world.

The author aims to show wherein this is true. He seeks to indicate and analyze those emotional states which most commonly disturb ministers and interfere with their work. Far from holding up the minister and his profession to ridicule, he would in the kindest way possible help the minister to see himself as others see him. Understanding oneself is the first step toward solving one's problems.

It is hoped that the reader will come to these pages with an open mind. The author writes out of wide experience and sympathetically, even when most searchingly. The reader, therefore, will do well to ask himself often, "Does this mean me?"

1

THE PROBLEM OF RESENTMENT

THE EXPRESSION, "the world, the flesh, and the devil," has frequently been used as a comprehensive description of all the foes which a minister must face. Which of these three is his stoutest adversary?

Contrary to what the minister himself may suspect, his toughest opponent, his most subtle temptation, may be resentment. Not the resentment which others may hold against him, but that which he holds against them; the resentment which he cherishes within himself, and which makes him both miserable and incapable of doing his best!

A true minister, quite rightly, will recognize the incompatibility of such a mental tone with the kindly, forgiving spirit demanded of him by his calling. But he may feel that to acknowledge the presence of resentment in his life would damage his ego. That ego, he contends, must be protected, defended, even though the doing of it may cost him his peace of mind. So it comes about, all too often, that actual resentment is rationalized as righteous indignation. Under this guise it is permitted to lie within the depths of this good man's personality, where it does extensive damage.

Resentment Against Those Whom He Serves

The minister may find it difficult to repress unholy bursts of anger against some leader in his church. Perhaps

9

his bitterness is directed against the chairman of one of the church boards, on the ground that this chairman has opposed, without cause, everything which he, as the minister, has sought to accomplish on behalf of the church. Or his resentment may be directed against certain individuals in the congregation who disparage or slight his earnest pulpit efforts. To him these individuals stand as symbols of frustration.

The reason for this, usually, is that the minister has equated self-aims with kingdom-aims. He seems unable to distinguish between the two. He assures himself, the congregation, and even the Lord that he is working and sacrificing solely for the benefit of the church, whereas he may be actually, though unconsciously, working and sacrificing chiefly for his own benefit. Thereby it becomes extremely difficult for him to be objective when he encounters opposition.

He has identified himself so completely with his work that he misinterprets any opposition to his plans for the advancement of the church. He takes such opposition as a personal affront. For example, he may feel that the trustee who opposes the building of a new wing on the church, or who objects to the purchase of a beautiful, but expensive, stained glass window, is for some reason working against him and trying to defeat him. Such may not be the case at all. This trustee, who thinks highly of his pastor and cherishes a warm regard for him, may honestly disagree with him concerning the thing he proposes to do. However, the pastor cannot see this, and the harm is done.

Similarly, it is not uncommon for a minister to feel a sense of dismay mingled with indignation as he watches his Sunday school leaders, teachers, and pupils troop past the sanctuary doors when the Sunday school has been dismissed. He has just heard them sing, "Our Sunday school is over, and we are going home." These words still haunt him when he comes to his study on Monday morning. Oftentimes he feels like running away from it all.

To be perfectly honest, it is not solely selfish egotism that makes him feel that way. He knows that he has a good, vital message, and that his people need to hear his sermons. He knows that he can answer their questions and indicate to them ways by which they can solve their problems, but they will have none of this. One pastor was asked by some of his young people to give them help with their intellectual difficulties concerning the Bible and their Christian beliefs. This pastor felt genuinely inspired to prepare a series of helpful messages. He worked out the sermons with care, but the delivery of them proved a profound disappointment. Not one of the young people who had asked for this help was present to receive it!

Sometimes the minister feels resentment because he is inadequately paid. A young and highly successful business executive once confided to the writer: "I often perceive the resentment which my pastor feels. I hear it in the tone of his voice; I see it in the glance of his eye. When he looks at me, he seems to be thinking, 'Yeah, you've got yours now, haven't you?'"

The underpaid preacher can hardly be blamed if he tends to feel resentful. His family budget is a battleground between income and expenses. All Christian workers pay a price to serve the Lord. Ministers expect this. But the relentless struggle to pay bills and meet debts plays an important role in producing the minister's emotional imbalance.

Finally, there is the continual threat and attack of criticism. He knows the hurt of it. But what pastor is there who has not had this experience? Let no pastor conclude, therefore, that he has failed above all others, if he feels this iron entering his soul. Every man of God must pass through his baptism of fire and drink his cup of bitterness. None is exempt from misunderstanding and misrepresentation. Members of his family must endure this criticism with him.

The Effects of This Resentment

If a minister yields to a spirit of resentment, a petulant tone will creep into his preaching. His sermons will become pitiful confessions of his dislikes, rather than the inspiring messages of peace, love, and confidence which his congregation needs.

The minister's sermon discloses the state of his soul. It reveals his spiritual poise or his inner turmoil. He cannot avoid this. His denunciation of sin may actually be a denunciation of certain sinners. In this way he seeks to compensate for his resentment and to release for awhile his stored-up anger.

A minister who had severely cudgeled his silent and unprotesting congregation had in reality merely verbalized his smoldering wrath against his position in life, a position which he felt had become intolerable. His tirade against unsound theology had been his way of saying: "I resent my position in life. I resent you. I resent my family. I resent myself. I am at war with myself." The scolding preacher is often a deeply disturbed preacher.

During the pinching days of the great depression, a young and immature preacher was guilty of at least one such sorry confessional. He felt resentful because the congregation that attended upon his pulpit ministry was small. He felt cheated, because there were many, so he believed, who could have found profit in hearing his sermons. Furthermore, he resented the fact that he had not risen at once to prominence in the community. He rebelled also against the stringencies of the times. He did not then understand the significance of all these feelings. That insight came only after many years, and therein lay the pity!

At any rate, this minister decided that he would frankly and courageously unburden himself. He would set matters right. He would do so by denouncing sin. He would disclose the stinginess, the indifference, and the neglectfulness of the members of his congregation. Perhaps he felt some promptings of caution, but he mistook them for signs of cowardice, and he moved on in his folly. His sermon, with its pitiful oratory, whined to an end. The congregation has listened patiently and politely. Perhaps a few were moved to sympathy for this mistreated young minister. Perhaps others thought furtively of their own unpleasant financial problems. Probably all of them left the church with a feeling of disappointment.

This foolish young preacher had prostituted an opportunity to bring to his congregation a message of inspiration and comfort. The people needed some word of encouragement from the Lord. They had not come to church to receive enlightenment concerning their pastor's plight. They had come for help with their own problems and perplexities, that they might the better face the bleak realities of everyday living. They desperately needed moral and spiritual undergirding. The young minister had not thought of this. He had been too busy thinking of himself!

This minister had sacrificed something fine in order to relieve temporarily his immature and overwrought emotions. But no one asked for his resignation. No one intimated that it should be forthcoming. There was no rebuke. Perhaps the church members felt that a rebuke would be useless. There was only disappointment and regret.

Another minister, one who enjoyed more than ordinary prestige, on one occasion devoted a considerable portion of his morning sermon to the development of the thesis that a congregation as affluent as his should provide their minister with a good automobile and a comfortable home. As he proceeded, it became apparent that his chief concern was for himself and his station in life. Probably he had long ago ceased to minister to the members of his congregation for their good. Instead of considering people as an end in themselves, he had come to consider them as a means to an end—that end being his own advancement.

Resentment makes a minister blind. This fact becomes apparent in the manner in which he administers the affairs of his church. Because he is blind, he cannot appraise people objectively and correctly. He no longer makes appointments on the basis of merit, but has resorted to a strategy of ostracism or exclusion. So far as he is concerned, church administration becomes a matter of putting his personal supporters in the positions of responsibility, and keeping out of those positions any who might oppose his plans. Kingdom interests are relegated to a secondary position.

Such a minister will be unable to see the good that there may be in his fancied enemies. He will be unwilling to make use of the abilities of those whom he considers opposed to him. In thus perverting his administration, he may actually regard himself as very clever. But the result inevitably is loss for the cause of Christ, for his luckless parishioners, and for himself.

The minister, of course, must use discrimination when appointing church leaders, for it must be acknowledged that often there are individuals who wish very much to occupy positions of leadership for which they are not qualified. They may lack ability and talent, or they may be so emotionally unstable that they would create chaos anywhere they might be placed. The point here is that the pastor should search his heart and not permit a feeling of resentment to influence him to discriminate against a person who is well qualified to fill an important church office.

Resentment will sour the minister's spirit. When he is resentful, he cannot preach as he should; he cannot pray as he should; he cannot counsel as he should. He keeps standing in his own light and is continually getting in his own way.

The harmful manner in which resentment operates is well illustrated in a letter received by the author from the editor of a well-known periodical for ministers.

"We know from long experience that you are touching upon the nerve-center of the actual drawbacks in the work of many, many men in charge of pastorates. If you could read the letters in one file here, bearing the simple title, "Amen," from men who work off their anger on us, when they cannot reach those against whom they bear resentment, you would better understand what I mean.

"We rarely allow any clerical worker in the office here to read such communications, or go near the file, because we learned some years back that young people who do are usually through with church attendance, not realizing that the letters merely express, psychologically speaking, a temporary blow-off which clears the air for the next few hours.

"It is a fact that many men have written the editor expressing the hope that his wife and family might have to sit in the public square and starve to death. Some even have written to our principal advertisers and turned their anger against us by enclosing what they claimed was a quotation from an article or letter in which, they charged, we had disparaged the advertiser's product, when as a matter of fact we had written nothing of the sort.

"In most instances these men repent and come with explanations of why they did what they did, when they need something very badly and are unable to secure it without our help.

"This has always been a mystery to us, since we wonder even now how such men can be in pulpits to preach to others on Christian virtues when they themselves are merely children in character-growth."

Resentment spreads like a contagious disease. It cannot be isolated. It infects the pastor's family. When the minister's grown son has an aversion to the church, it may be due to his father's inner disturbance.

The members of the minister's family, because of their sympathy for him, may not be able to see events in proper perspective and proportion. When a parishioner gives offense, instead of recognizing that shortcomings characterize all human beings, they fancy they see a malicious intent and a deliberate breach of Christian conduct and attitude.

In this matter the minister cannot see his own culpability. He cannot see it because he does not wish to acknowledge it, and because he prefers to transfer to some convenient person the onus of his failure. Thus, to his own satisfaction at least, he explains away those failures and mistakes which are unacceptable to his ego. This is the most insidious and dangerous aspect of resentment. It blinds the minister to his real problems and their proper solution, and it does this at the very time when he most needs spiritual insight.

A minister who cherishes resentment hurts those whom he should be helping. Some of his displeasure inevitably spills over into the lives of those who love and trust him. As he communicates his ire, he destroys something vital— the faith which the laity have in him. The minister may not know this, because at the time his only concern is to relieve his feelings and enlist sympathy.

In like manner, his wife and the other members of his family are constrained to share their grievances with solicitous friends, both within the congregation and outside it. In the warm sympathy which they feel when in the presence of trusted friends, they find it impossible to keep from voicing their angry frustration. They make strong charges which may or may not have a basis in fact. The result often is that parishioners are alienated from the church for many years or even for life. If parishioners are thus affected, how much more detrimental is the minister's resentment in its effects upon those outside the church circle! What a stumbling block in the way of those who, at one time or another, may have contemplated uniting with the church!

Overcoming Feelings of Resentment

The minister, more than any other man, must know himself. He must penetrate the insulation of self-esteem. He must see himself as he really is. Above all, if he finds himself habitually feeling slighted, neglected, and mistreated, he must learn to view his feelings with suspicion. Such self-examination calls not only for wisdom but also for courage.

He should remember that one of the strong motivations for human behavior is the preservation of the ego, and that he, although a minister, is as concerned to protect his self-esteem as other men are. Everyone feels bound to cling to his self-pride as long as he lives. It is for this reason that the most difficult words for any man to say are, "I have been wrong." They are hard to say because they reflect on the integrity of the self and on the wisdom of the mind. They are equivalent to, "I have sinned."

It is feared that the minister too often is disinclined to acknowledge personal and specific wrongdoings or wrong feelings. Such a confession, he feels, would destroy his congregation's belief in his integrity, or would weaken their trust in his wisdom. It seems to him important that he foster the myth of perfection. However, he must be as honest with himself as he would have others be with themselves. He must have the courage to analyze his own motives and conduct.

The minister, then, should see in his displeasure an inadvertant admission of imperfection and guilt, and in his resentment a psychological mechanism which he employs vainly to absolve himself from this imperfection and guilt.

The words of Jesus are appropriate here:

> "Why do you see the speck that is in your brother's eye, but do not notice the log that is in your own eye? Or how can you say to your brother, 'Let me take the speck out of your eye,' when there is the log in your own eye? You hypocrite, first take the log out of your own eye, and then you will see clearly to take the speck out of your brother's eye (Matt. 7:3-5).

The minister must understand that a chronic state of resentment is an unhealthy frame of mind, one which is closely related to other forms of mental illness. He should realize that his mental and emotional life is not functioning properly if he habitually reads evil-intent into the words, actions, and attitudes of others; if he nurses the suspicion that disparaging remarks are being made behind his back;

or if he is quick to believe that there are conspiracies against him. It is true, of course, that people discuss the minister. It is true also that at times they discuss him in an uncomplimentary fashion. But do they not, in similar fashion, discuss their children's schoolteachers, the mayor of the city, the aldermen, and the chief of police? To lend an ear to such reports, except to wring from them whatever benefit one can, is to aggravate self-pity, which in itself is harmful.

It will be well for the minister to remember that although he has unkind critics, he has also many loyal followers, in whose prayers he is constantly mentioned. Let him heed the advice given by the apostle Paul; namely, to meditate on the things that are beautiful, true, pure, and of good report. Then the God of peace will be with him.

The minister may not realize that the resentment which he feels toward his congregation is only another evidence of his dependence upon his congregation. It is a curious but well established fact that the poorly adjusted minister feels the need for congregational support more than does the well adjusted minister. Many pastors, to be happy in their work, must be assured and reassured of the esteem in which they are held by their congregations.

Some psychologists hold that this desire for praise is one of the fundamental dynamics by which men live. They view it as a drive for power, a drive which operates below the level of consciousness and which measures its success by the praise and honors received. Other psychologists attribute this desire for recognition to a pampered and thwarted childhood. Some see the motivation as remote; some see it as current and immediate. There probably is some truth in each of these views. We are dealing here with a compensatory drive toward self-realization—a drive which is beneficial if held within limits, but which is harmful if allowed to go beyond them.

The minister, early in his career, receives almost universal adulation. People have a tendency to overpraise a young preacher. His earnestness, his sincerity, and his bright promise attract people to him. In their friendliness and enthusiasm, they feed his ego too much. He cannot mature as he should, if he is constantly showered with praise. He is tempted to presume upon his gifts. If he yields to this temptation, his life remains stunted emotionally, mentally, and spiritually.

As a result, he retains all his life a profound need for praise. He feels he must receive it in order to maintain his self-esteem; otherwise he cannot live with any degree of satisfaction. Unwittingly, he permits himself in this respect to become dependent upon his congregation. If he does not receive from his congregation reassurances with reasonable regularity, his self-esteem ebbs away. He becomes unaccountably depressed. Obviously, the minister ought not to allow himself to become thus dependent upon the praise of men.

The minister, being mortal like everyone else, must have recourse somewhere. He wants something on which to lean. More than any other man, he must learn to depend upon the solid Rock of Truth; he must cultivate the Unseen Presence of God. God must be to him a living Reality. Otherwise, he will become a cynic.

The praise of men is as uncertain as the wind, and the man of God is a fool to lean upon it. It can easily and unexpectedly shift. Men's derogatory remarks also are like the wind, and just as apt to change their direction. The man of God is foolish to be dismayed by such criticism. Neither praise nor blame is stable; neither gives a true picture of a man's worth.

The true measure of a man's worth is to be seen in his own deep and unassailable sense of integrity and rectitude. A man knows in his own soul what his true worth is. Here, the wise observation of Charles Haddon Spurgeon, the great London preacher, has point:

"I have striven with all my might to attain a position of complete independence from all men. I found at times, if I have been much praised and if my heart has given way a little and I have taken note of it and felt pleased, that the next time that I was censured and abused I felt the censure and abuse more keenly; for the very fact that I accepted the commendation rendered me more sensitive to the censure. So that I have tried, especially of late, to take no more notice of man's praise than his blame, but to rest simply on this truth: I know I have a pure motive in what I attempt to do, to serve God with an eye single to His glory; and therefore it is not for me to take either praise or censure from man, but to stand independently on the rock of right doing."

A congregation does not exist to serve its minister. He exists to serve the congregation. He exists to comfort and strengthen others, not to be comforted and strengthened by others. This is the lot of the man of God, because it was also the lot of his Master. "The Son of man came not to be served but to serve, and to give his life as a ransom for many" (Matt. 20:28). We are told also: "A disciple is not above his teacher, nor a servant above his master" (Matt. 10:24).

In dealing with criticism that hurts, the minister will be wise to ask himself, "Are these things really true that people say about me?"

People sometimes understand the minister better than he thinks they do, better—it may be—than he understands himself. It is difficult for a man to see himself as others see him. He cannot know how he impresses others, or what his influence upon others is. For this reason, a man must always remain to some extent a stranger to himself. But it is possible for a man to learn valuable truths about himself from his detractors. Others can see his shortcomings more clearly than he can. If he will take account of their criticism, he can turn it to good account. In that way he can make his critics serve him.

To shut one's ears to criticism in order to escape unpleasantness is unwise. One can learn more from adversity than from prosperity. It may be that the only way some men can learn anything is through pain. In dealing with criticism and using it to one's advantage, one must wisely appraise it before accepting it or rejecting it. Men do not always speak the truth about the minister, but sometimes they do. The minister, therefore, should give heed. Above all, he should stop, look, and listen when he finds himself involved repeatedly in the same kind of unpleasantness.

When Abraham Lincoln was told that his Secretary of War had called him a fool, he remarked: "If Stanton says I'm a fool, I must be one. I had better go and talk with him about it." Charles Haddon Spurgeon also had the happy faculty of profiting from adverse criticism. He had been in the habit of saying, "Nothing in my hand I bring." An anonymous letter-writer in a caustic note reminded him of this fact and observed, "We are now sufficiently informed of the vacuity of your hand." The great London preacher laughed and said, "He was a valuable aid to my progress."

Criticism is an inevitable fact of life, and the minister must accept it. The very nature of his message makes opposition certain. If he withstands low ideals and injustice, if he proclaims the full word of God as he should, he is bound to feel the sword. In fact, he should beware when all men speak well of him. If he gains universal popularity, it may be because he has not done his whole duty.

There is a perversity in human nature that sometimes makes men rebel against the truth, but there is an imperative in faithful preaching that demands the truth. This truth must be proclaimed if people are to be saved. If the Master did not escape the cross, how can the faithful minister expect to do so?

The minister must accept criticism without rancor. A wise mother once said to her preacher-son: "Be chaste as ice, as pure as snow, thou shalt not escape calumny." That preacher-son had to taste this bitter truth without any alleviation, except that furnished by his inner assurance of integrity.

"Taking up your cross," wrote John Ruskin, "is carrying whatever you find is given you to carry as well and stoutly as you can, without making faces or calling people to come and look at you. All you have to do is to keep your back straight, and not think of what is on it. . . . Above all, do not boast of what is on it."

The minister must learn to understand people sympathetically, if he is to help them and, at the same time, save himself from bitterness. This does not necessitate compromise. Some ministers, unfortunately, feel that they would be compromising with evil if they were to relent and entertain thoughts of conciliation or sympathy. These are the men whom time breaks.

"Always be kind," said Ian MacClaren, "for everyone you meet is fighting a hard battle." Truer words were never spoken. Back of the placid faces of the morning congregation, back of the offhand remark and the casual approach, are problems and battles which are terrifying. In these turbulent times, people are fighting the battle of their lives to keep poised and sane.

When the prophet Ezekiel went down to Babylon to preach to the captives there, he had in his mind only words of denunciation, but when he "sat where they sat," he was astonished. And God said to him, "I have made you a watchman." (See Ezek. 2:8—3:17.)

Jesus saw men as lost sheep, as lost coins, as prodigal sons, as builders on sand, as weary and heavy-laden. Some measure of this sympathy must actuate the man of God. He must see as other people see, feel as they feel, labor as they labor. He must pray for understanding of them. His ministry must be that of the broken heart and the tear-filled eyes. This is the spirit that saves and serves.

People are much like children. They seek for someone who will understand them, believe in them, and love them in spite of their imperfections. They must feel an acceptance that does not demand of them perfection or complete tractability.

The minister, therefore, must make allowances for the inevitable imperfections of the people whom he has been called to serve. There is no redemption in denunciation; there is redemption and healing only in love. In the case of the restoration of the demoniac of Gadara, the healing factor, aside from the divine power, was the infinite tenderness and love which Jesus showed him.

Imperfection is concomitant with human nature. People are not perfect and never can be in this life. They can be better, but not perfect. Perfection is an attribute of deity. God alone is perfect. A church is a society of the imperfect.

It is, possibly, one organization among men which requires an acknowledgment of imperfection of those who apply for membership.

The minister sometimes overlooks this fact. He assumes that laymen will be perfect, and resents it when they are not. Their shortcomings excite his anger instead of his sympathy. He expects from them a pattern of life and a consistency of conduct which are difficult, if not impossible, even for himself.

The pastor is called to labor with human beings who often are poorly adjusted to life and who are driven hither and yon by frustration, apprehension, and anger. A non-Christian lawyer once remarked that church people often had trouble among themselves. A discerning minister replied: "That is to be expected. The church attracts imperfect, disturbed people, for it offers them that which they feel intuitively they need."

Jesus indicated this fact when he said: "Those who are well have no need of a physician, but those who are sick; I have not come to call the righteous, but sinners to repentance" (Luke 5:31-32). If a pastor finds in his parish persons whose lives are incomplete, ill, or neurotic, let him not languish or be dismayed. Such persons are encountered everywhere. There is work for him to do.

Instead of reading his own resentment into the lives of those whom he would serve, the pastor must learn to understand and love them. To do this he must continually face himself and his God. He must know himself first, in order that he may come to know others.

"Young man," a benevolent pastor once said to a seminarian, "when you get into the pastorate, you will find people who will misunderstand and oppose you. You will be disposed to strike back, but you must not. You must take them into your heart and love them."

It is said that George Fox, the founder of the Society of Friends, endured without resentment all the cruelty and malice heaped upon him. When struck while preaching, he did not strike back. He merely wiped the blood from his mouth and went on preaching. He saw a great ocean of love overflowing a land of darkness.

Charles Kingsley, able preacher as well as novelist, was noted for his tenderness of spirit. This tenderness was born out of his deep reverence for the human soul. Someone remarked that while Kingsley may have smiled at the foibles of people, he never was known to have sneered at anyone.

The minister needs the quality of patience. Many aggravated situations will yield only to the healing touch of the hand of time. The wise minister waits on the Lord and bides his time. He knows that truth has a way of vindicating itself, and that sometimes a cause may be lost because a man insists upon running ahead of it. By pressing for verdicts and by forcing the issues, one may succeed only in making bad situations worse. There is something in human nature that will not be coerced. If a man is permitted to yield of himself, he will do so more quickly and more completely. Therefore, "in your patience possess ye your souls" (Luke 21:19, KJV).

2

THE PROBLEM OF IMMATURITY

IF A MINISTER feels resentment, it often can be attributed to immaturity—the immaturity of character which he discerns in those whom he has been called to serve, and the immaturity, alas, which they in turn discern in him. Although resentment due to immaturity of character does not differ greatly from other forms of resentment, the problems raised by such immaturity are of sufficient importance to deserve separate consideration.

In every church organization of any size there will be persons who have achieved physiological maturity without having achieved psychological maturity. These emotionally immature persons can best be understood as children. They have not reached that maturity of character which shows itself in a steadfast love for others. Indeed, they may as yet be incapable of unselfish love. They are motivated by feelings of resentment, bitterness, and envy. They may react toward the pastor much as a stubborn child does toward an authoritarian parent. Their words and attitudes may be marked by a self-assertiveness which in reality is merely their attempt to bolster their egos.

Sometimes such persons transfer to their pastor bitter feelings which they have come to hold toward God. If they feel that God has been responsible for their losses or misery, then the pastor, as God's representative, is likely to receive the brunt of their rebelliousness. If he attempts to give them assistance, they may heap on him their inner turmoil and resentment.

The minister, however, cannot permit himself to react to others in the manner in which they react to him. His heart must be compassionate and tender. His insights must be tempered with mercy. In short, he must love. It is not enough for him to understand people; he must love them. This requires him to be a saint. Difficult? Yes. But the world needs saints!

An Immature Attitude Toward His Calling

Many a minister is like an eager, untried knight of old. Upon entering his first pastorate, he sallies forth in a spirit of idealism to do combat with sin and injustice. It is good to be idealistic, and it is good to do battle, but it is not good for the minister to be naive and immature in his outlook.

Frequently the youthful preacher does not count it enough to be a preacher; he feels it incumbent upon him to become a *great* preacher. To be a good preacher, of course, is a legitimate aim. To be a great preacher is something quite different. The youthful preacher may feel that it is his destiny to minister to the multitudes, and he becomes impatient if that goal cannot be reached immediately. He hopes to become a tremendous force for good, one to be reckoned with in his time. He feels that he cannot be content with anything less.

Perhaps the young minister should not be blamed overly much if this is his aim. The nature of our culture is largely responsible for such ambitions. We worship bigness. Nothing seems really great unless it is large and noisy. In popular opinion, the great preachers are those who command the attention of vast crowds, who fill the famous pulpits, and who receive large salaries. We find it difficult to equate greatness with humility and patient labor in an obscure situation.

The youthful preacher, accordingly, longs for the day of his greatness to arrive. He labors and frets and waits. The years inexorably roll by. His hair becomes sprinkled with gray. Then, one day, he awakens to the fact that more than half his life has been spent and his dream has not yet been fulfilled. He realizes, perhaps for the first time, that it may never be fulfilled.

As he looks about him, he sees young preachers who already have achieved what he had hoped to achieve. He assures himself that he is just as capable as they are, and probably more deserving. He feels that time, for some reason, has played a mean trick on him. Furthermore, he sees young men in other walks of life who already are enjoying that affluence and social recognition which have been denied him.

Then comes a major crisis. He sees even more clearly how little of life's ambitious dream will have fulfillment. He is confronted with the fact of his mortality; he sees the futility of the meaning which he has been reading into life; he experiences the frustration of being just a little too old.

The minister, at such a time, is tempted to cynicism. He may become a sullen victim of self-pity. He may surrender to discouragement or despair, and so be irretrievably lost to the ministry. Or he may fail to perform that very considerable good which he might do, if only he could reconcile himself to service in some less conspicuous and less remunerative post.

An Immature Attitude Toward His Colleagues

The minister's immature attitude toward his calling is sometimes extended to include his colleagues. It is most unfortunate if he allows their greater success to arouse in him any spirit of resentment. The minister's resentment sometimes is directed toward his predecessor. Upon entering a new pastorate, he may take an unholy delight in circulating reports that reflect upon the moral, intellectual, or financial integrity of the pastor who preceded him. He may petulantly refuse to extend to him the courtesy of the pulpit. Such an attitude would be amusing, if it were not so tragic. The shortcomings of such a minister are not lost upon discerning laymen, but are seen by them as indications of emotional immaturity.

A minister of this sort has not progressed very far beyond childish rivalry, strife, and egocentricity. Yet it is quite likely that in his preaching he will stress the necessity of being born again, of being changed from an ego-centered man to a Christ-centered man. It is quite likely also that he will stress the importance of sound doctrine. It is easier to preach sound doctrine to others than it is to practice sound doctrine in one's own life.

It will readily be seen that a minister who falls short in these respects is psychologically immature. He is resentful because he feels inferior. He fears that his own work will not compare favorably with the work which others have done.

Too often the individual attempts to rationalize his feeling of resentment. He seeks to absolve himself of guilt by transferring the blame to another. A certain pastor, on entering a new field, found the work difficult. Not long

afterward he met his predecessor in a public gathering, and
to that man's great surprise immediately and most unfairly
began to berate him and to blame him for certain worldly
attitudes which he said he had discovered among the young
people in the congregation.

Often a minister finds himself greatly irked by a holier-
than-thou attitude displayed by one of his colleagues. This
is especially true if the holier-than-thou preacher, in a tone
which plainly says, "I've got something which you do not
have," piously and solicitously informs him that he sym-
pathizes with him in his hard situation and will be praying for him. Considerable poise and forbearance are required to summon the gratitude expected in return for the
promised prayers.

Much Christian forbearance is called for when one must
deal with such a supercilious colleague. He may be the
pastor of the largest and most aristocratic church in the
community. Because he has become prominent in civic
and community affairs, it is easy for him to fall into a
pompous and condescending manner. He comes to regard
himself as the ultimate in ministerial accomplishments.

When such ministerial friction is combined with the
divisive denominationalism and rivalry which have become
our tradition, we have a situation which is most unwhole-
some. It is small wonder that the man on the street queries,
"Why don't the churches get together?"

Growing in Christian Character

It is now high time to consider what may be done to
overcome the immature attitudes which keep the minister
from being at his best. What are the highways which lead
to growth in Christian character?

*Every minister needs to watch his motivation constantly,
and whenever the need arises he should be prepared to
purge his motives of all selfishness.* There is bound to be
some frustration at this point. However sincere one may
be, it may prove impossible to divorce all personal concern from one's motives. To be completely selfless, one
would need to be dehumanized. There is likely to be an
element of self in even the most altruistic act. However,
this element of self can be held in check and disciplined.
It must not be permitted to get out of hand. It must not
be allowed to become the dominant motivation in one's
life.

If the minister is to render significant service and live at
peace with himself, he cannot permit self-concern to become
his chief concern. In this respect the ministry probably is
more demanding than any other vocation. The pastor's
usefulness depends upon his motivation. Why did he enter
the ministry? If his motives were ulterior, he cannot successfully disguise them throughout his entire lifetime. Perhaps for a time he can conceal his true motives, but every
disguise in time wears thin. The ministry demands complete sincerity. It demands humility—a humility that for-
gets itself as soon as it is born.

In the minds of laymen, the ministry connotes service,
sincerity, and humility. This is wholly in accord with the
mind of Jesus. No affectation or superficiality will pass
muster. If a man is not willing to be sincere, humble, and
faithful to his work, he should not be in the ministry.

A young man's reasons for entering the ministry must
be valid. It is not enough for him to agree that they should
be. They *must* be. Without being aware of his real motives, he may choose the ministry because he sees in it an

opportunity to advance himself, to be the center of attention, or to wield considerable authority. He believes he will be looked up to, respected, or even idolized. He expects to receive certain favors and special consideration. He anticipates that through being in the ministry he will escape some of life's hard experiences. In other words, his real reasons for choosing the ministry are selfish ones.

If this be the case, he is headed for disillusionment. His call to the ministry must be authentic and his motivation must be unselfish. A "search for glory" will not eventuate in satisfying achievement, and an egocentric spirit will succumb to the discouragements encountered in a pastorate of any considerable duration.

A valid call to the ministry is a call to serve one's fellows without any consideration of oneself. It is a call to be a pastor as well as a preacher. It is a call for the shepherd heart. Something stirs within the person—something that would lead him to express himself at the bedside of the sick as well as from the pulpit. Seized by such a call, one does not wish to manipulate people, but to help them. The true pastor wishes to help them find their places in life and to assist them in achieving the full development of their personalities. He does not wish to set people straight in an authoritarian manner; instead, he wishes to lead them, even as a shepherd leads his flock.

It sometimes happens that even though a young minister begins his career with a lofty purpose and an irreproachable aim, the years do something to him. The world's philosophy may penetrate his armor. Crass indifference and leaden apathy may dull the keen edge of his zeal. The hypocrisy which he discovers in high places may dampen his enthusiasm. The grim economic conflict may divide his heart.

The faithlessness of his fellows may make him cynical. In consequence, he may admit compromise into the citadel of his inner life and so prepare the way for more serious declensions. Pride may delude him. His environment may overwhelm him.

It is not surprising, therefore, that a minister sometimes will yield to disillusionment and come to resent the calling which now he cannot forsake. The years prove to be against him. He retreats into the shell of professionalism and expediency. If he emerges, it is as a sophisticated cynic.

Although Dr. Albert Schweitzer, in his youth, had found a comfortable, happy, and successful place in life, he was restless and dissatisfied. "It struck me as incomprehensible," he has explained, "that I should be allowed to lead such a happy life, while so many around me were wrestling with care and suffering. When I awoke one morning and birds were singing outside, I settled with myself before I got up that I would consider myself justified in living until I was thirty for science and art, in order to devote myself from that time on to the direct service of humanity. What would be the character of the activities thus planned for the future was not clear to me. I left it to circumstances to guide me."

Eight years later he found on his writing table the magazine of the Paris Missionary Society. Opening it, he read an article describing the needs of the Congo mission.

"The article finished," he said, "I quietly began my work. My search was over."

Shortly thereafter he enrolled as a student of medicine and pursued the prescribed, arduous course. When he had completed it, he journeyed to a remote and needy section of French Equatorial Africa.

"It was my answer to Jesus' saying," he declared, "that whosoever would save his life would lose it, but whoever would lose his life for the sake of the gospel would find it."

Of the friends who tried to dissuade him, he said: "They could not conceive that a desire to serve the love preached by Jesus would sweep a man into a new course of life." He said also: "There are no heroes of action. There are only heroes of renunciation and suffering. Anyone who proposes to do good must not expect people to roll stones out of his way, but must accept his lot calmly if they even roll a few more upon it."

In these words Dr. Schweitzer has described the spirit which should motivate every minister. That spirit *must* motivate him, if in the future he is to escape disillusionment and frustration.

The wish to succeed, of course, is woven through the whole fabric of human nature. It is a healthy wish, but the man of God may need to purify his conception of what constitutes success. Success cannot be stated in terms of the rewards promised by a materialistic philosophy. If it is, the man who so regards it is destined to become a cynic. The minister who cannot think in terms of God's will rather than his own will should seek another calling. If, however, he can think of success in terms of a humble effort to elevate human life, then an ever-increasing richness and happiness of spirit will become his possession.

The minister is not called to be great. He is not called to be brilliant. He is not called even to be successful. He *is* called to be faithful.

Every minister needs to learn the potential of the seeming inconsequential. An illustration or two will make this clear.

There was a time when a pastor with the right spirit, even a very obscure one, could have been of great help to George Fox, who eventually became the father of the Quaker movement. At twenty years of age, this sensitive mystic left his little shop and went off in search of a remedy for the ills of the world.

First, he went to the priests for guidance. He should have received help from them, but he did not.

"Get married," said one.

"Become a soldier," advised another.

"Take a physic," counseled a third.

"Use tobacco," suggested a fourth.

Why should they bother to give sound, spiritual advice? This queer lad was a nobody. Their time was too valuable to be wasted on him!

Out of those unhappy experiences, George Fox learned a lasting contempt for professional clergymen.

There was a time, likewise, when a pastor with understanding and insight, even an obscure one, could have been of great help to the youthful Francis of Assisi. Francis was desolate, deep in the brooding that accompanied the formulation of his life's plan. When he sought help from the religious leaders, none would aid him. All were too busy with their own interests. They felt that Francis did not merit attention. He was unimportant and queer. Besides, he was visionary and disturbing.

No one ever knows how significant a seemingly inconsequential service may prove. An obscure pastor became an inspiration in the life of George W. Truett. Another obscure man, one who was not even a minister, brought about a turning point in the life of Charles Haddon Spurgeon.

It is the pastor's privilege to direct the course of human personalities. Although many of the lives to which he ministers may never achieve renown, all of them can achieve real worth. Many a pastor who is working at the grass roots of society, although overlooked because he is located in some remote rural area or because he is hidden in the heart of a teeming metropolis, is performing a service too great to be measured. These pastors who labor day after day, unknown, unpraised, unsung, are truly men of God. How poor the world would be without them!

When ministers think constantly of the limitations of their lot, they are tempted to become petty and irritable. They fret because they do not have a feeling of accomplishment. They resent spending their lives in ministering to only a few. They dream of large congregations and the thrill of achievement. They commiserate themselves because of their bondage to trifles, and through their irritability they endanger their usefulness. At the same time, they make themselves miserable.

Our Master did not feel that he was too important to render lowly service. Some of his most profound utterances were made to obscure individuals.

"God is spirit," he said to a woman of doubtful reputation, "and those who worship him must worship in spirit and truth."

"Unless one is born anew," he explained to a man whose name would not have come down to us had it not been for his meeting with Jesus, "he cannot see the kingdom of God."

"On this rock I will build my church," he announced to a hardy fisherman, "and the powers of death shall not prevail against it."

At the conclusion of his profound Epistle to the Romans, Paul remembers twenty-four persons by name and sends them greetings.

In a class in theology, there was a discussion of this fact.

"How can you explain it?" asked one student. "Why did Paul blunder with so many postscripts at the end of his letter?"

"My dear young man," replied the professor, "it was because of his interest in these persons that he wrote the letter."

The apostle Paul reminded the Ephesian elders that he had kept back nothing that was profitable for them, but had taught them publicly and from *house to house.*

Once a pastor was busy in his study. He was deeply immersed in preparing what he believed would be a great sermon. While in the heat of composition, he heard a knock at the door. What should he do? Ignore the knock and go on with his important task, or go to the door and get rid of the caller?

Remembering in time what the work was that he had been commissioned to do, he went to the door. But even so, as he opened it, hasty, irritable words trembled on his lips.

There stood a middle-aged man who diffidently held his hat in his hands.

"I am sorry to disturb you at this hour of the morning," the man said in a low voice, "but I had to come. All night my wife and I were unable to sleep. We need a minister to help us. I have come to ask you to help us find God."

Every minister needs a humble spirit. Without it, he is in danger of succumbing to the same temptations which overcame the scribes and Pharisees of old.

Of these scribes and Pharisees, Jesus observed: "They do all their deeds to be seen by men . . . and they love the place of honor at feasts and the best seats in the synagogues, and salutations in the market places, and being called rabbi by men. But you are not to be called rabbi [Hebrew, Great One], for you have one teacher, and you are all brethren. . . . Neither be called masters, for you have one master, the Christ. He who is greatest among you shall be your servant; whoever exalts himself will be humbled, and whoever humbles himself will be exalted" (Matt. 23:5-12).

Jesus' stern warning was against pride. Pride renders a man vulnerable to pain and corruption.

Alexander Maclaren, throughout his ministry, retained his pure zest and zeal. He kept himself free from all traces of envy and bitterness. Early in life he had learned the valuable lesson of humility.

"I thank God," he once said, "that I was stuck down in a quiet little place to begin my ministry."

The chapel at Southampton had eight hundred seats, but the congregation had dwindled to fifty. "During the first five years you could have had a pew to yourself and another for your hat!"

This great expository preacher never did gain complete confidence in himself. Often, when finished with a sermon, he would exclaim: "It is over. How I managed I cannot tell. I did my best, and I must leave it there."

He cared nothing about news reports of his appearances, and he discounted heavily all the flattery heaped upon him in the days of his successes. His happiest moments were those in which he was carried along by the stream of sermon delivery. His most miserable moments, before and after those efforts.

A biographer states: "When one listened to his easy flow of graceful language, his fastidious choice of the precise word, one might think it was a natural gift, but such was not the case. In his early years his delivery was slow and halting. He often paused to select the exact word to express the right meaning."

His humility was his power.

Another distinguished English preacher, Frederick W. Robertson, despite his eloquence and saintly life, never held a high office. During his brief ministry (he served only four churches) his humility kept him from seeking high position.

A discerning observer remarked: "He was not plastic enough in the hands of the powerful to gain preferment. He had the insight to see that a man might lose the power to be a bishop in the act of gaining the office. He would not sacrifice the interiorities of life to save its exteriorities."

A pastor, speaking from experience, once observed, "A long-continued pastorate is beneficial to a minister in that it purifies his motives, teaches him adaptation, and develops his self-control.

"Ministers need to study the motives that actuate them," he continued. "They need to ask themselves, 'Why am I trying to do this work?' They cannot sustain enthusiasm for souls and intellectual force apart from motives that have wearing power. In a lengthy pastorate all motives wear out except holy ones. It will never do for a long-time pastor to be other than a good man."

"I bid every one among you," writes the apostle Paul, "not to think of himself more highly than he ought to think, but to think with sober judgment . . ." (Rom. 12:3). Paul's admonition has lost none of its timeliness.

*Every minister needs to deal positively and constructively
with any unworthy motives and feelings which may arise.*
As has been implied, the cross which the minister is required to carry is more than one of adversity or opposition.
It is a cross on which he must crucify all within himself
that is unchristian. The inner struggle is never easy, but
there are ways by which the victory can be won.

A consecrated and successful pastor has given this account of his way of overcoming the jealousy he was tempted
to feel toward his predecessor. "I make it a point," he said,
"to invite my predecessor at least once a year to return
and speak from my pulpit. This helps to keep me from
becoming petty and jealous. When I feel that spirit rising
in me, I crucify it in that way."

Surely the minister should regard his colleagues as co-
workers in a divine calling. Each is an imperfect work-
man, to be sure, but so also is he himself. Let him view
all of them fairly; let him see them, not through the
jaundiced eyes of suspicion, but through the clarity of good
will. Quite possibly the man he dislikes is also driven by
fear. He too may be fighting a hard battle under this self-
assured and exasperating exterior.

Most certainly, the man of God should pray. Prayer is
his strongest support, his ever-present resource. Prayer will
purge his soul of envy. You cannot continue to bear ill will
toward one whom you are lifting by name to God in prayer.

F. B. Meyer, the well-known London clergyman, once
was invited by Dwight L. Moody to come to Northfield for
a series of conferences. He was welcomed with enthusiasm
and immediately became very popular. However, a few
days later, the renowned expositor, G. Campbell Morgan,
arrived on the scene. The large congregations that had

waited so attentively on Dr. Meyer now turned to Dr. Morgan. It was a trying experience, and the spirit of Dr. Meyer no doubt was sorely tested. He acknowledged later that he had been strongly moved to be jealous and resentful.

"The only way I could conquer my feeling," he confessed, "was to pray for him. Which I did."

3

THE PROBLEM OF INFERIORITY FEELINGS

ANOTHER INNER ANTAGONIST against which the minister may have to contend is his fear of being thought inferior. This fear produces feelings of insecurity and frustration. The minister who has such a handicap is filled with apprehension, because there lurks in his mind the belief that someday the mask will be torn away and he will be found out for what he really is. Inferiority, his true status, will then be boldly written out, and all will see how miserably he has failed to measure up to their expectations.

This inner disquietude may make him uneasy in the presence of other ministers, some of whom may occupy pulpits of greater prominence than his own or who may be given to a freer airing of their ideas. This same disquietude may make him reticent or ill at ease in the company of men in other walks of life who have achieved some measure of success or who seem very sure of themselves.

Possibly such a minister consoles himself with the thought that his peculiar personality or position produces this estrangement and renders it difficult for others to understand him. It is conceivable that in some instances this may be true, but it is more likely that the estrangement is of his own making. It may result from his fear that he is not able to measure up to others. He hesitates to

43

express himself lest he appear inept or ridiculous. He does not want others to reject him or to think less highly of him through having discovered his inadequacies. Thus, he continues to feel inadequate; and this outcome is largely due to the fact that he has judged himself to be inadequate.

The Origins of Inferiority Feelings

The origins of such apprehensions are many and varied. Some affirm that the causes are to be sought in the remote influences of childhood. This, of course, would be the analysis made by those who belong to the Freudian school of thought, and it must be recognized that there is much validity to this theory. Many of one's fears and resentments can be traced back to patterns which were established in childhood by influences then playing upon one's life.

There are other psychologists who contend that in order to understand a man's problems, one needs to look at the present. They hold that man is born with a will to power, and that his destiny is to work out his self-realization as best he can. A person's conduct, they say, must be interpreted in the light of his drive to self-realization, and his success must be judged in relation to the obstacles thrown against it.

Certainly there is validity in this position also. Problems are born in the present as well as in the past. The pressures of the present impinge upon the sensitive areas created by the past, and thereby make one what one is. To maintain that all of one's problems may be traced to childhood influences is an unwarranted acceptance of determinism.

Although those who are disinclined to face life and shoulder responsibility sometimes appeal to psychological determinism as an excuse for their numerous shortcomings, it doubtless is true that some apprehensions had their beginnings in the psychological splits which unfortunately occur in many households.

Joseph Parker, the renowned London pulpiteer, grew up in a divided home. His childhood was one of hardship and stern conflict. There arose an estrangement between himself and his father. His mother's love for him was the one salutary influence in his early life. Although he found a measure of compensation in the ministry, he remained always a sensitive adult.

Such psychological splits induce feelings of insecurity in the mind of a child. They make him uncertain as to his actual status as a person. Some ministers, no doubt, have had unhappy childhoods of this sort. The sacred calling of the gospel has drawn them because of the compensations which it offered. It promised them fulfillment and self-realization.

Some apprehensiveness may be due to the fact that one's early life was very humble. Many ministers have come from rural areas, many out of the ranks of working people. This is not to their discredit, but rather to their credit. However, since human nature is what it is, and since our culture is what it is, this humble origin may have left them with some feeling of self-disparagement.

Very few ministers have come from wealthy families. Many of them have had to live meagerly all their lives. They have been forced to forego even the more moderate luxuries of life. Some have had to perform menial tasks and practice rigid discipline in order to secure college and seminary training. After much rigid economy and self-denial, they have become settled in small pastorates which, in many instances, have necessitated a continuance of the very same economy. Because there is a direct relationship between a man's salary and his self-respect, inadequate remuneration is a prolific cause of self-depreciation.

The minister knows that although he may be only a twenty-four-hundred-dollars-a-year man he should not feel embarrassment when associating with a fifteen-thousand-dollars-a-year man. He knows that he has a high calling and that his value to society is not measured by the amount of his salary. But it is easier to manage one's mind than it is to manage one's emotions. Adequate financial remuneration is more than a means of livelihood. It is a source of self-respect.

Ministers in the smaller denominations are especially susceptible to inferiority feeling. One may not suspect this, so sure of themselves do some of these ministers seem. Nevertheless, they are acutely aware of the disparagement with which they are regarded in some quarters, and they react to it with suspicion and acerbity. Unconsciously, they are on the defensive. Their problem is rendered the more acute when they are aware of their deficiencies in the matter of academic training.

The same sort of feelings sometimes exist between those belonging to the so-called high church and low church parties, between those who hold ecclesiastical position in high esteem and those who do not.

Inferiority feelings may arise also from a belief that one's moral endowments are less than those of others, or from a belief that one's early sins, long since repented of, are still being charged to one's account. We know how intense was the struggle within the soul of Paul. He repeatedly reproached himself for the sins in his past. He could not blot out the memory of having persecuted the church of God. Because of those sins, he called himself the least of the apostles.

Indications of Inferiority Feelings

Feelings of inferiority reveal themselves in various ways. Curiously, their presence sometimes is indicated by the very efforts put forth to conceal, disguise, or disown them. Such attempted deception has many ramifications and may take any one of several forms.

For example, it may be observed in a pronounced tendency to flatter people. Flattery may be the means which the minister would use to bring under a measure of control those whom he fears or in whose presence he feels inferior. In assuming this role, he may consciously or unconsciously be seeking to manipulate people by showing them special attention. Evidence of this may be detected in the abundance of public praise he showers upon certain individuals in his parish. This is not to maintain that public recognition should never be given. In some instances, the praise will be merited; in other instances, it will not. The praise, in the latter cases, will be simply a bid for some reciprocal favor.

A discerning parishioner once said of his minister: "He is only trying to flatter us. I believe that is the only way he knows by which to manage people." The observation appeared to be true. The minister under discussion possessed talent and ability, but he underrated himself. Because of his feeling of inferiority, he had employed flattery rather than honest commendation. Thereby he had exposed himself to suspicions of insincerity. It is obvious, therefore, that indiscriminate, highly colored flattery may have no effectiveness. Indeed, if it creates suspicions of insincerity, if people begin to say that the minister does not mean what he says, but is using flattery for the purpose of manipulating people, then it acts as a boomerang and is highly dangerous to the minister.

Furthermore, inferiority feelings are a prolific source of plagiarism. Sometimes preachers have stolen other men's sermons because they were too lazy to prepare their own, or because they had permitted other interests to crowd out the work of sermon preparation, or because they did not like to think creatively. However, when a minister has yielded to the temptation to use a sermon not of his own preparation, it usually has been because he suffers from a feeling of inferiority. He believes that the appropriated sermon is better than anything he himself could prepare.

Such a minister reasons within himself that he could never word that particular thought so beautifully and effectively. "Why not use it?" he asks himself. "After all, there is nothing new under the sun. So long as I make it my own, what harm is there?" The harm is twofold. In the first place, plagiarism eventuates in deterioration. If a man does not use his own talent, that talent will be taken from him. In the second place, plagiarism does serious injury to one's opinion of oneself. The preacher who preaches another person's sermon without acknowledging his indebtedness soon loses his self-respect and also his self-confidence. In consequence, his feelings of inferiority are confirmed and deepened.

Ministers who are given to such a practice never become truly emancipated. Instead, they become more and more dependent upon other men's thoughts. Their sermons become a hodgepodge of other men's sermons. Sometimes experiences related as being their own are in reality only digests and adaptations of experiences which others have had.

A lecturer representing an international philanthropic organization related a number of humorous anecdotes. He told them as his own experiences. One of his stories had him preaching in a church. At the conclusion of his address, one of his hearers approached him and said: "I didn't know you were a minister. Are you?" "No," laughed the man, enjoying himself hugely. "That was just a story."

May we not find here one key to the skepticism with which many discerning persons regard the pulpit and the utterances that pour forth from it? How is the listener to discern between fact and fancy, between truth and fiction, between honesty and dishonesty. Will not the average churchgoer before long ask the question which the minister's little daughter put to her father after he had told her a story. "Daddy," she said, "did that really happen, or is it just preaching?"

When a minister is addicted to borrowing ideas from other preachers, he may reach the point where he is afraid to launch out upon his own. He has tried to be someone else for so long that he has failed to become himself. He cannot think for himself, and for that reason he cannot respect himself. He is loath to trust his own talent.

Sometimes this unfortunate apprehensiveness manifests itself in an unduly assertive manner. A certain amount of aggressiveness, of course, is normal and beneficial; but a minister who feels himself to be inferior, in his efforts to cover up that fact, very frequently will carry his aggressiveness too far.

Some ministers have the unpleasant habit of relating impressively all of their accomplishments. They boast of

the gains their church has made in membership and attendance. Perhaps the reason the preacher who wants to mo-
nopolize the conversation with a glowing account of his
importance proves irritating is that the listener wants to talk
about his own importance!

Often a minister seems so self-sufficient, so self-assured,
so capable, so courageous, so militant that a layman is not
likely to suspect that inwardly he is apprehensive. Such a
minister appears ready to do battle with any adversary, at
any time, and at whatever cost. He is the first to scent
heresy and to expose it. He does battle nobly in the arena
of doctrine. He does not hesitate, even from the pulpit,
to name his enemies. He builds up straw men with amaz-
ing skill and tears them down with withering zeal!

When such a minister steps in to take over a meeting,
he assumes command with an air that says: "Well now,
things are going to happen, and they are going to happen
the way they should happen!" But the very stridency of
his voice betrays the fears he would conceal. The quaver-
ing inner voice cautions: "You can't do it. You're not equal
to the occasion." The booming outer voice, however,
shouts: "Oh, yes, I can." It may be that the more uncertain he is of himself, the more loudly and emphatically
he speaks.

Such a person may write letters to unsuspecting ministers,
asking them this plaintive question: "Brother, I'm a puzzled
sinner. I don't know the way of salvation. Won't you
please write me, telling me what that way is? Make it
absolutely clear, so that I may understand completely."
Then, having received the answer, he immediately declares
it to be unscriptural and proceeds to have a field day of
exposure and denunciation.

Yes, some preachers have done just that!

Such an unhappy, much-to-be-pitied soul is never sure of himself. He moves from parish to parish, always trying to run away from something or to find something better, always confronted with situations he cannot cope with, always involved in what he thinks are insurmountable difficulties. He withdraws in defeat too soon. To his fear-filled soul, life is not a co-operative, benevolent enterprise, but a bitter conflict in which he has been beaten.

Another indication of inferiority feelings is a tendency to refuse to participate in various undertakings. This is the logical consequence of a fear that one is not equal to meeting the situation or the person confronting one. It involves an avoidance of feared or resented individuals and of the meetings at which they are likely to be present.

Hence, the minister may consider it inexpedient to co-operate with other ministers in community affairs or events sponsored by a union of churches. He may protest that he is a very busy man, and this protest may serve to revive his wilting self-esteem. Or he may base his refusal to participate on an avowed concern for doctrinal purity. He may insist that he cannot afford to associate with ministers whose beliefs are nebulous or are open to question.

What he actually does is to withdraw into his own bailiwick, where he can assume undisputed command, and where his compulsion to feel important goes unchallenged. In his own little world he can bask in the light of his own reflected glory, free from any annoying misgivings.

Such tendencies are cumulative. One withdrawal calls for another, and the ultimate result is great loneliness.

Furthermore, feelings of inferiority may manifest themselves in extreme sensitiveness. We are not to conclude from this statement that nothing can be said on behalf of sensitiveness. The minister must have a sensitive spirit, if he is to make fine distinctions and sense the variations of mood he finds in human emotions. He must be as sensitive to people and situations as a musician is to nuances of tone. If he is to deal helpfully with human beings, he must be capable of feeling the movements of mind and spirit. He must be sensitive to life. He must be capable of empathy as well as sympathy. That is to say, he must be able, by imagination, to project his consciousness into that of another. In this sense, sensitiveness is a spiritual gift.

There is a point, however, at which sensitiveness ceases to be of value and becomes a hazard. It then is no longer a spiritual endowment, but becomes a mark of personality disturbance. It has been said that a man should suspect himself when everything that happens injures his pride. Such oversensitiveness may indicate deficient vitality or an unhealthy and fearful emotional life.

The overly sensitive minister flares up at unexpected times and in inappropriate places. He is piqued by a suspicion that his status is being challenged. He is nettled by the thought that his jittery self-esteem is in danger. Therefore, he resorts to aggressiveness to cover up his inner fears. A person usually is not sensitive unless he feels unable to cope with life.

A small-town pastor once caused a short article to appear in the local weekly newspaper. It told of a missionary of his denomination who was to speak at his church one evening that week. It concluded with the statement that the public was invited to attend the meeting. Another minister in that community—one who was quite busy feeling sorry for himself—thought he detected in the news story an effort to proselyte. Accordingly, he addressed to him a scathing letter, saying: "You have no right to do this thing. It is just another evidence of your unduly aggressive policy in this town." No doubt in later years he regretted having written the letter. This same oversensitiveness worked against this minister in his other pastorates. Had he overcome it, his ministry would have been much more effective.

Then there is the preacher who tries to be sensational. He may engage in attempts to be spectacular. He may indulge in the bizarre. He may court publicity. Or he may try to be a funny-man. By such efforts he usually succeeds only in making himself obnoxious or ridiculous. The hearer soon gets the feeling that such a preacher is only playing a part. In reality, the preacher may think himself to be inferior, and he has assumed this role because it strikes him as being impressive and commanding.

Such a minister resorts to tricks and stunts to build up his drawing power. He advertises such sermon subjects as: "Did She Jump or Was She Pushed?" The first personal pronoun may be emphasized throughout his sermon, and there may be a colorful description of his dramatic exploits.

This preacher operates on the theory that people lack discernment. He thinks they cannot see that in trying to make them laugh, he actually is endeavoring to draw attention to himself. Instead of trying to be humorous, he should be doing them good by making them think and feel deeply. It has been said, "Never underestimate the ignorance of an audience." That is valid advice for the minister who is fond of displaying his erudition, but it is faulty advice if it is accepted as a dictum. It is not a true appraisal of the listening public. The superficial attitude which many a

preacher has toward his congregation has led many intelli-
gent people to adopt a skeptical attitude toward all pulpit
utterances.

At the opposite extreme from the spectacular is the pose
of erudition. This is no reflection upon genuine scholarship. There is a place for it. However, it should be observed that the truly great scholars are humble men who
are not given to showing off. Usually it is the person who
feels inferior in the matter of education who does that.

This type of "show-off" employs a barrage of fanciful
phrases, Greek quotations, and unfamiliar and imposing
words. Small wonder that so many sermons drift over the
heads of the listeners! A truly gripping sermon is one that
answers deep-seated questions in the minds of the hearers.
But these sermons answer no questions, because they never
come to grips with life in terminology that has meaning
for those who are seeking help.

Such sermons are not made for the people, but for the
clergyman himself. Without realizing it, he phrases them
in a manner designed to bolster his ego and enhance his
self-respect. Secretly he may be thinking, "If I make this
material sufficiently erudite, I shall gain the respect of the
people. They will consider me intellectual and learned."
So he trifles with the esthetic; he traffics with the oblique;
he indulges in catch phrases; or he delivers a psychological
lecture—all the while dwelling on the periphery of things,
instead of dealing in simple language with the matters of
greatest urgency. In seeking to appear learned, he fails
to make clear the help which the faith he espouses has to
offer.

Sometimes the wish to appear modern will lead him to
preach sermons based on the most popular books. This

is not to say that the minister always should avoid the best-sellers. Assuredly, he should be conversant with the literature of his day, as well as with the literature of the past. He must have some acquaintance with the current books, if he is to judge correctly the spirit of the times. The point is that he should not make these books a substitute for the insights and imperatives of the Scriptures.

Eternal truth should not be appraised against the backdrop of the best-seller; rather, the best-seller should be appraised against the backdrop of eternal truth. Best-sellers are a current phenomenon; the Scriptures are everlasting. The minister who feels under necessity to appear clever and sophisticated may be seeking the praise of men rather than the praise of God.

Dispelling Feelings of Inferiority

Many of these fears are groundless. What a relief many ministers would feel if only they could realize this!

We know that some of the ablest ministers have suffered such qualms when there was no reasonable basis for them. Alexander Maclaren probably was such a person. It is said that he never gained complete self-confidence. Even in the days of his renown, he was nervous over special sermons and addresses. He gained no confidence from the brilliant record behind him.

Joseph Parker was another. He was extremely distrustful of himself and yearned for some visible indication of his effectiveness. He lived in constant need of encouragement. For this reason, he was often taken to be an egotist. The apparent egotism, however, was only a mask for his extreme diffidence. He gave the impression of being overbearing because he was lacking in self-confidence. Although he seemed impervious to criticism, he was in reality very sensitive to it. The feelings of inadequacy which oppressed him were without foundation. Great throngs heard his sermons at City Temple. Everyone knew of the excellence and worth of his ministry, but he remained always distrustful of himself.

The minister will do well to prepare himself adequately for his calling. This statement is prosaic and unromantic, but it is important. Adequate preparation is vital to his calling; it is vital to himself.

There are men who wish to be ministers, but who are unwilling to pay the price required of those who would be good ministers. Occasionally one finds a young man who seeks ordination without first having completed an adequate course of study. There are churches that will "lay hands suddenly" on any eager and persuasive aspirant to the ministry.

This is not to place training above sincerity, but to say that sincerity should provoke a desire for thorough preparation. The pastor needs both sincerity and learning, and both are in view in a legitimate call. Sincerity must be buttressed with adequate learning, if the minister is to be ready. He needs theological, philosophical, and psychological training; he needs to be versed in biblical interpretation and church administration, if he is to feel sure of himself. Sincerity fortifies scholarship, and scholarship fortifies sincerity.

The young aspirant to the ministry should be satisfied with nothing less than complete college and seminary training. Years ago the writer was brought to this decision when he received a letter from a wise, elderly pastor who wrote: "Be sure to get full seminary training in addition to your college training. It will strengthen you immeasurably." The full value of that advice was not appreciated until some years later, when the seminary training had been secured and the sobering experiences of life had given some new insights.

It is probable that many ministers feel resentment and inferiority because they realize that they are inadequately prepared for their work. Although they may have done much in the way of self-education, their lack of formal preparation for the ministry deprives them of the self-assurance which they need.

Basically, every pastor needs a proper respect for himself and for his calling. Tendencies toward flattery, retreat, and pose usually are attributable to self-disparagement. Self-disparagement, even when paraded under the pseudonym of humility, is neither good religion nor good mental health.

Every minister, regardless of who he may be, possesses something intrinsically fine in his make-up. He has at least one talent. That talent must not be lost through fear or self-disparagement. Instead, let him discover it and use it. In the familiar parable of the talents, one man lost his talent through not putting it to use. The minister may be in danger of making the same mistake. He preaches this truth to others; why should he not see its application to his own life? This may be the reason Paul advised the youthful Timothy to have respect for himself and his calling. He bade him not permit anyone to despise his youth. The pastor's temptation may be to take too low a view of himself.

Although the Christian is reminded not to think of himself more highly than he ought to think but to think soberly, there certainly is nothing sinful in a healthy self-respect. The writer recalls with gratitude the chapel messages delivered by Dr. John F. Herget, then the president of William Jewell College. One bore upon this point. Dr. Herget, in his simple, direct fashion, related the ancient account of David's combat with Goliath. He described the hurried efforts of Saul, the king of Israel, to prepare David for the contest by dressing him in his own oversized, kingly armor. He pictured the ludicrous sight of the slim lad engulfed in the heavy helmet and breastplate. Then, in language that stuck, he related the skill and deftness of David who, choosing to depend upon his own resources, knelt at the brook in the valley, selected therefrom a few smooth stones, and with his sling—his own familiar weapon—felled his huge, lumbering adversary.

It is feared that ministers sometimes venture upon the battlefield while cumbered with the weight of armor that is not their own. They employ weapons with which they have no skill when they should make use of their own talent, whatever it may be.

A plea which is often heard is, "I do not have the time." This excuse calls to mind some challenging words of Alexander Whyte, who by great perseverence had mastered a defect in verbal memory and achieved eminence as a preacher. "We cannot seriously look into one another's faces," he said to a group of ministers, "and say it is want of time. It is want of intention, determination, method, motive, conscience, heart. It is want of anything and everything but time."

One of the wisest admonitions of all time is, "Know thyself." Another is, "Be thyself." Shakespeare, in *Hamlet,* has Polonius declare:

"This above all: to thine own self be true,
And it must follow, as the night the day,
Thou canst not then be false to any man."

To yourself be true; that is, be true to your truest and best self. There is no one else just like you. No one else has exactly the talent that you have. No other can do *your* work, the work you can do by *being yourself*. So do not try to be somebody else. Release yourself by being yourself, by preaching your own message.

Some men have been brilliant performers, yet their work has not endured. Their names have been forgotten. Other ministers have had only a brief career, yet their memory lingers. The reason lies not so much in what they did, as in what they were. There was in them a certain fineness of fiber, achieved through their respect for their true selves.

It is travail of soul, combined with fidelity to the truth within himself, that gives the man of God authenticity and true worth.

One of the best ways to deal with inferiority feelings is to begin a serious, spiritual work with individuals.

Let the minister honestly become concerned for the needs of people, and let him consider what he can do to help them. Let him think of them as persons. Then he will be less inclined to think of his ministry as an achievement to be made impressive. Let him think of his ministry as a cure of souls, a blessed work which he can perform, if he will. Thereby he will come to a higher evaluation of his work and of himself as a minister.

Let him return to the neglected and frequently ridiculed work of soul-winning. Let him devote himself to a spiritual ministry directed toward individual persons. If he does this without any thought of personal advantage, he will come to possess a new and wholesome sense of mission and worth. The evidence of changed lives will do more than anything else to bring him the assurance he needs. It will be beneficial to him personally, because he will be doing his distinctive work—the work of an evangelist—and thereby fulfilling his ministry. However, he must do this work, not for his own sake, but for the sake of others.

An Episcopal rector once remarked: "To be vitally in contact with individuals whom one is trying to draw to Christ tones up all of the minister's study and devotional life. Many a man I know could have been saved a bad case of spiritual indigestion, if he could have been helped to combine his studies with a constant, redemptive touch with people."

Occasionally a minister will judge himself to be inferior because he is making demands on himself that are too rigid. That is to say, he may feel under compulsion to be absolutely saintly, absolutely self-controlled, absolutely patient, absolutely successful. But these are idealistic goals, never fully attained in this life.

Sometimes a minister, without realizing it, sets an impossible goal for himself. He feels he must be able to endure everything. He feels he must be able to like everybody, be able always to do his best, be always productive, never be ruffled, and never feel hurt. To have done merely what is good is not enough for such a perfectionist. But no one ever realizes these goals except in his imagination. The result is discouragement and self-disparagement. The minister must appraise himself soberly, not too optimistically and not too pessimistically. He must try his best to be objective when passing judgment upon himself. Adequate and healthy self-respect demands it.

The minister's aim should not be the winning of glory. The desire for glory, when one surrenders to it, becomes insatiable. Neither should it be self-respect through the attainment of perfection, for that is humanly impossible.

It will be sufficient if his aim is constant growth in Christian character and service. The apostle Paul, having affirmed that his supreme aim in life was to "gain Christ and be found in him," went on to say: "Not that I have already obtained this or am already perfect; but I press on to make it my own, because Christ Jesus has made me his own. . . . I do not consider that I have made it my own; but one thing I do, . . . I press on toward the goal. . . . Let those of us who are mature be thus minded" (Phil. 3:12-15).

The adequate life, free from feelings of inferiority, demands self-control. This is obvious and trite, but true.

It is not enough simply to be aware of the facts. One must do something about them that is positive and constructive. The minister needs to bring himself into line. "For God did not give us a spirit of timidity but a spirit of power and love and self-control. . . . Take heed to yourself and to your teaching; hold to that, for by so doing you will save both yourself and your hearers" (2 Tim. 1:7; 1 Tim. 4:16). A pastor, so Paul wrote to Titus, must be "master of himself, upright, holy, and self-controlled" (Titus 1:8).

Joseph Parker, to whom reference already has been made, was a man possessed of such contrasts of temperament that he had a severe inner conflict. With him it was either self-mastery or self-defeat. He suffered periods of depression during which he contemplated abandoning everything, but he persevered until at last he achieved self-mastery. It became apparent to those about him that he was growing steadily with the passing of the years, and that his work was growing with him. The secret of his growth was, first, his mastery of himself, achieved by directing all his powers to that desired end, and, second, his wholehearted giving of himself to people of all classes. Such an achievement demands determined exercise of the will, for only thus does a man work out his salvation.

The minister must permit the mind of Christ to dwell in him. He must endeavor at all times to live a life surrendered to the will of God.

He cannot serve two masters. If he tries to do so, he will be in constant trouble and most unhappy.

A pastor, smitten with a sense of personal futility in trying to follow two careers, uttered these anguished words: "Would to God I had given myself wholly to the ministry twenty-five years ago!" If the minister would be free from feelings of inferiority, let him cease thinking of himself and trying to serve himself, and let him think of mankind and, as a minister of God, serve mankind to the best of his ability.

F. B. Meyer, pastor of Regent's Park Chapel, London, and Christ Church, Lambeth, once declared: "I have no special gifts. I am no orator, no scholar, no profound thinker. If I have done anything for Christ and my generation, it is because I have given myself to Jesus Christ, and then have tried to do whatever he wanted me to do."

4

THE PROBLEM OF DOUBT

ALTHOUGH HIS MANNER may not indicate it, the minister, like everyone else, is subject to periods of depression. At such times, doubt insinuates itself into the deep places of his being. The extent to which it gains control will vary with the individual, but it is safe to assert that at some time or other doubt has assailed every pastor. Even such notable ministers as Joseph Parker, Alexander Whyte, Alexander Maclaren, Charles Haddon Spurgeon, Adoniram Judson, John Mason Peck, and Horace Bushnell did not escape the subtle intrusions of doubt.

The Forms of Doubt

Doubt may arise at any one of several points. For example, the minister may be troubled with doubt as to his calling.

There are times when it appears to him that he would have done better to have chosen almost any calling other than that of the ministry. He becomes acutely aware of his deficiencies and failures, and he reproaches himself that he did not leave so exacting an occupation to those who are specially gifted for it.

Dr. George W. Truett once remarked that every Monday morning he felt like resigning. Discounting the evident facetiousness of his words, one can see in them an

63

undercurrent of feeling that makes brothers of us all. There are, indeed, distressing times when a minister will question whether he was actually called to the gospel ministry. He may reproach himself for having permitted the exuberance and idealism of youth to sweep him into a calling for which he seems to have so little talent.

Furthermore, there are times when he is sorely tempted to doubt the efficacy of the gospel which he has been called to proclaim. He has been asserting that the basic validity of the Christian faith lies in its power to impart a transcendent dynamic, a power capable of changing life, of checking its downward tendency, and of empowering it for nobler living. He has preached this fact, but some of his failures make him question the power of the gospel to effect such a salutary change. He reflects also that although he has given himself completely to his work and has preached as faithfully as he knows how, the people in his congregation seem to be no better than they were. His message seems to have proved ineffective.

As he views the matter in his darker moments, the people sit passively in his church Sunday after Sunday. They listen apathetically to his earnest expositions of the gospel of redemption. The benediction is pronounced and the people file out—to pursue the unaltered tenor of their ways.

Week after week he counsels the distressed, the fearful, the confused, the selfish, the erring. He gains a measure of insight into their problems, but he perceives that usually they reject the truth concerning themselves. He sees them place the blame for their failures and unhappiness on others. They continue blindly in their former manner of life.

It occurs to him that usually people approach him, not for insight and advice, but for official sanction on a course they already have determined to take. If he counsels them to do what they *want* to do, they are pleased and call him good, possibly wise. If he counsels them to do otherwise, they are disappointed, displeased, and possibly call him narrow and biased. Many people are like Ahab, the king of Israel, who complained of Micaiah, God's honest prophet: "I hate him, for he never prophesies good concerning me, but evil" (1 Kings 22:8).

Many times the pastor feels that about all he achieves by his counseling is an *appearance* of conformity and piety, instead of the genuinely altered life he would like to see. He concludes that people are more concerned about appearing to be good than in actually being so.

"What's the use of preaching?" he asks himself. This is no idle question. There is real pathos in it. There are times when he feels a deep kinship with Jeremiah, who had to watch the blind rebellion of his people against God, despite all his warnings, pleading, and tears.

The minister is tempted to cynicism when he sees the fickleness and superficiality of people, their predilection for the sensational, their disinclination to accept truth which disturbs their prejudices, their disposition to call that which pleases them "good" and that which displeases them "bad." He sees the easy wrong chosen in lieu of the hard right. He sees their blind spots with respect to morals. He wonders if his ministry is worth the effort. He feels that at best he can be but a feeble voice crying in a very great wilderness.

His assurance concerning the efficacy of his ministry is further assailed when he hears a social worker assert that people with personality disturbances should be referred only to well trained psychiatrists. It is inferred that a minister could not possibly have anything helpful to offer. He re-members having read of a day when religion wrought mental healing, and he wonders what has changed the situation. Likewise, he hears a case worker say that pastors should refer cases of domestic strife and problems involving shame to a qualified consultant, on the ground that the persons involved, after having revealed their intimate, personal affairs to the minister, will not wish to return to church. Accordingly he wonders what has happened to the cure of souls, and if there is such a thing any longer.

This is not to discredit the worth of psychology and psychiatry to human society. They have been of invaluable aid to understanding and health. The minister should welcome and study the insights provided by these sciences, but he should not permit them to magnify themselves to such an extent as to lead him to question the worth of his office. Doubt on this matter is profoundly distressing, because it denies the minister's philosophy of life and questions the strategy which he pursues. It attacks the validity of the cause to which he has given his life and from which he cannot honorably turn away. Let him be assured, then, that there is still a valid and supremely important place for the pastor in our present-day society.

Sometimes a conscientious minister will wonder if even he himself is sincere. He sees his own selfishness injecting itself into the pastoral or preaching situation. He sees evidences of his own ulterior motives. He questions whether he can ever be as sincere as he should be, or as humble, or as selfless.

All the above are strong statements, but probably they do not exaggerate the doubts entertained by many ministers, at least in the more discouraged periods of their lives.

The Causes of Doubt

Why should these doubts exist? If the minister is living as he should, why should he be subject to these recurring times of depression?

The minister, of course, is only a man, and often only a very ordinary man. He is not a superman. Neither is he an iron man. He has feelings and emotions, the same as other men; he grows weary, even as others do.

Often the minister's doubt can be traced to weariness or ill health. It is difficult for the spirit to be optimistic when the flesh is weak; it is difficult for the spirit to be full when the emotions are empty. A minister may suffer from doubt because he has not been as mindful of himself and of his reserves of strength as he should have been. He may be depressed simply because he is worn out. Literally, he may have poured himself out so completely that he has become physically, emotionally, and spiritually drained.

There is a logical and close relationship between nervous fatigue and mental depression. Elijah, after his strenuous contest with the priests of Baal on Mount Carmel, became dubious about the loyalty of his people to God. He had won the contest, but it had left him depleted in spiritual strength. He became plagued with the fear that he alone was faithful to the Lord. The reason is obvious. He had passed through a time of tension in which everything had been at stake. There had been a high pitch of emotional excitement. After the excitement came the reaction, swift and hard.

This sort of emotional depletion has come to countless religious leaders. People, by and large, do not know how much emotional drain there is upon the apparently uneventful life of a pastor. They do not realize that this emotional drain reduces one to exhaustion more quickly even than manual labor. Many a minister, after he has officiated at a funeral or has spent long hours in a difficult counseling situation, feels that he has been run through an emotional wringer.

Phillips Brooks, with his massive body, seemed the personification of inexhaustible strength and courage. But when he became a bishop, his energy was exhausted by time-consuming engagements, and his superb physique was taxed to the utmost by the rigors of continuous responsibility. He discovered that he was always depressed when he was overworked. Similarly, Charles Haddon Spurgeon, with all his hardiness of spirit, was miserably depressed when his physical energies were drained.

Thus the minister may be seized with doubt concerning himself, his calling, and his people simply because he has given himself to them without reserve. His health and vitality are then at a low ebb. He has had little rest. Indeed, he cannot rest; because he feels he must continually be at his work. More than such a minister may realize, his close association with people and their problems has been a drain upon him. He suffers vicariously. Without his realizing it, power has gone out of him in making others more confident.

An attack of depression, therefore, does not mean that significance has dropped out of his ministry, or that he has made a mistake in choosing his life's work, or that the fight against the devil is futile. It may only mean exhaustion.

Some of the minister's doubts may arise from the fact that he is not permitted to know the full extent of his usefulness. People often do not think to tell a minister when

they are being benefited by him. This situation is due in
part to the fact that people find it difficult to express that
which they feel deeply. If the average minister knew the
full extent of his usefulness, he would be both surprised
and much encouraged.

A pastor was invited to attend a civic club dinner at
which the speaker was a prominent, retired industrialist,
just returned from a fact-finding tour of postwar Germany.
He had occasionally attended the minister's church.

When the speaker arose, he said, "I do not think that
Reverend M— knows this, but he is partly responsible for
my trip." The minister was amazed. "A few months ago,"
the speaker continued, "I attended a service in his church.
It was the beginning of the year. I had just retired from
active service in my firm, and was trying to decide what to
do in the future. I was feeling a little blue and discouraged.
Then the invitation came to go to Germany and make this
study, and I wondered if I should accept the invitation.

"That morning his sermon subject was, 'The Land of
Beginning Again.' In his sermon he made four points. I
have taken those four points as a guide for my life, and
I have repeated them many times as I have traveled and
spoken across the country. 'To enter the Land of Beginning Again,' Mr. M— said, 'a man must have vision, faith,
courage, and action.' His sermon helped me to decide what
I should do."

That experience was a revelation to this minister. He
could remember the occasion. He could recall seeing the
man seated in the balcony, quietly listening. But there had
been no indication whatever, either during the service or
afterward, that the sermon had had any effect. So, a minister never knows what he has accomplished, and probably

it is better that he should not know. If he knew, he would either be so elated by praise that others could not live with him, or he would be so depressed by criticism that he could not live with himself!

In some cases the minister may find the source of his doubt in an unsuspected invasion of secondary and secular interests. His mind may have been diverted by attractions, demands, and pulls that were foreign to his calling.

Normally the minister is a shepherd of souls. His distinctive function is the spiritual oversight of the flock. However, in the modern situation, he finds he has to be many other persons. He must be a business executive, a director of finances, a contractor, a building supervisor, a promotional director, and a public relations man. He is expected to affiliate himself with service clubs and to be active in community affairs.

Now, it is laudable that his talents and temperament are such that his fellows have confidence in him and should wish to put public responsibility upon him, but what of his distinctive vocation? There is ever-present the possibility that his soul may become preoccupied with secondary interests and that the secular will crowd out the spiritual.

The minister may be aware of what is taking place, or he may realize only that conditions within himself are not as they should be. Whether comprehended or not, the fact remains that he is subject to these distractions. Secular concerns invade his life and he is beset by conflicting interests. It is then that he begins to doubt the efficacy of his calling.

Such a minister is not "tenting" in the right direction. As the days swiftly pass, he finds that he has less time for meditation and prayer, less time to read the Scriptures for the nourishment of his soul, less time to maintain contact with spiritual realities, less time to live and move and have his being in God.

When one meets such a minister, one is depressed by the realization that here is a man who has lost his sense of mission, his reason for being, his grasp on the spiritual dynamic of which he should be the personification. He bustles with activity, his life is filled with many things, but the deep, silent springs within him have dried up, and it is futile for men to come to him for spiritual refreshment. Once he was a source of power. He could move, compel, sway men. He could with assurance point men to God. He was a blessing to all. But now, high-powered materialism has smothered the bright flame. He is no longer a confident man of God. He doubts.

Perhaps it will come as something of a shock to such a minister to perceive that whereas he has lost much of his faith, prominent laymen today are beginning to talk earnestly of vital truths, of a back-to-God movement to redeem and preserve society, and of man's profound need for something deeply spiritual.

A minister will become a prey to doubt if he loses the conviction he once held that the gospel is fundamentally relevant to human need. How he came to lose that conviction, he cannot explain. By degrees, almost imperceptibly, he left it behind him. While he was "busy here and there," it slipped away. Thereafter he may offer an occasional tribute to it as a fine ideal, but his words are empty.

Perhaps he has come to the conclusion that the gospel is outmoded and that psychiatry has more to offer to society. Psychoanalysis may appear to be more reasonable than prayer. Contemporary writings may seem to be more realistic than the ancient Scriptures. This is not to say that the minister should avoid these fields or be unversed in them. Certainly he should not discount the scientific study of human personality. Rather, this is a warning to the minister —a warning lest he forget that he is primarily a man of God, and come to despise his birthright and the distinctiveness of the Christian gospel. If he does not take care, he may reach the point where he feels officially committed to a faith that no longer has meaning for him.

Doubt may also be caused by hidden, unacknowledged sin in one's life. Isaiah gave forceful expression to this truth:

"Behold, the Lord's hand is not shortened, that it cannot save,
  or his ear dull, that it cannot hear;
 but your iniquities have made a separation
  between you and your God . . ." (Isa. 59:1-2).

Men lose faith in God, not so much because of honest doubt as because of dishonest sin.

A brilliant educator possessed what seemed to be a firm faith in God and a wide knowledge of eternal truths. He could speak beautifully of his faith. Then he lost his faith. In a shocking address, he said: "Christianity is now outmoded. It cannot save the world."

What was the reason for this sorry declension from faith? The reason was not long in coming out. He had begun to have immoral relations with a woman. The decay of his morals, very obviously, was the basis for the decay of his faith.

More than we realize, perhaps, our desires determine our thinking. The psychologists tell us that we repress our vagrant desires into the subliminal region of our minds that they may escape detection. Also we may attempt to

rationalize God out of the scheme of things, because God
and our sins cannot exist side by side. Hence, a man may
be unable to find God, because in reality he does not wish
to find God. He does not wish to find God, for he cannot
think of God without realizing that God reproves him for
his sins.

Dispelling the Insidious Doubts

How, then, shall the minister dispel the doubts which
beset him?

*To begin with, let him learn the homely efficacy and
genuine piety of rest.* It is positively wicked for a minister
to deplete his priceless reserves of strength by unremitting
toil, day and night, week after week, year after year. Such
a course is wicked, not for the minister only, but for every
man. The minister, to be sure, must be conscientious about
his work. There is no substitute for such conscientiousness.
But he can be conscientious to a fault.

The pastor of an active, metropolitan church may refuse
to take a vacation. Also he may decline the services of an
assistant, although his congregation offers him that help.
Perhaps they perceive, as he does not, that he is undermin-
ing his health and shortening his life by his constant and
taxing labors.

What manner of egotism is this that drives a man on to
his own destruction? Is it that he wants to prove to himself, as well as to others, that he is indispensable? The
cemeteries are filled with persons who thought they were
indispensable!

Let the minister learn the valuable lesson of rest, relaxation, and play. Let him learn to make himself and his
spirit sit down. He should not labor until physically and

spiritually exhausted. Let him heed the Fourth Commandment: "Remember the sabbath day, to keep it holy. Six days you shall labor, and do all your work; but the seventh day is a sabbath to the Lord your God; in it you shall not do any work . . ." (Ex. 20:8-9). Neglected sabbaths have a way of collecting compound interest after a man has reached forty.

It is well for the minister to take a regular vacation every year. Even better, so some ministers think, are two shorter vacations during the year, possibly one in the summer and the other during the winter.

Furthermore, the minister should set aside a regular time for relaxation and rest during the week. If he can arrange it so, it is wise for him to rest at some time on Saturday, preferably on Saturday afternoon. In this respect, at least, it is well for him to be a sabbatarian. Rest on Saturday will be more beneficial to his Sunday efforts than rest on Monday. He will then come to his biggest day of the week at the time when he is in his best physical condition. On Sunday morning he should be rested and relaxed.

It is the opinion of the writer that the minister's sermons should have been prepared before Saturday. He may wish to review them or to prepare a final draft of them sometime on Saturday, but it would be extremely perilous and presumptuous to wait until that late day for the initial inspiration and thorough preparation of them. Some homiletical geniuses have been able to compose sermons on Saturday evenings, or on their way to church, or even between the church door and the pulpit, but the average preacher is not so gifted.

The minister, if need be, should learn to play. Whether he be young, middle aged, or old, he will find that regular periods of play on the golf links, the tennis court, the volleyball court, or the handball court, will do much do reduce his waistline and dispel his pessimism. In physical exercise—of course, it should not be engaged in to a dangerous extreme—the tensions are relieved and the emotions are released. The mind actually is washed by the good natured give-and-take of play.

Some men feel that they have no time for play. The likelihood is that they have set for themselves an impossibly heavy schedule of work. Even if they hurry, they cannot do all that there is to be done. Not in one lifetime! Not even if they drive themselves relentlessly day and night throughout their entire lives. A man, by foolishly trying to do this, succeeds only in consuming his energy and depleting his reserves of strength to such an extent that the length of his service will be seriously diminished.

"One of the surest marks of greatness," observed Robert Louis Stevenson, "is accessibility, and the appearance of having an unstinted allowance of time. Extreme busyness, whether in school, kirk, or market is a symptom of deficient vitality; and a faculty for idleness implies a catholic appetite and a strong sense of personal identity."

The minister should organize and budget his time as carefully as he organizes and budgets his income. He finds his mind relieved when he has budgeted carefully the money that comes to him. He then knows at all times where he is financially and where he is going, and thereby escapes many worries. The minister's time is even more valuable than his money. By budgeting his time, he will get more work done and he will get it done better. He can then relax with more ease of mind, when the time for relaxation comes.

A major point in the philosophy of the famous Christian physician, Sir William Osler, was that a man should live one day at a time. He would have him cut himself off from the dead yesterdays and the unborn tomorrows, and live, as best he can, the day which is at hand.

So the minister should live his life—one day at a time, one task at a time. Let him do well the task in which he is engaged, without carrying into it the tensions created by the task which preceded it or any anxiety for the task which is to follow it.

Ministers move quickly from sorrow to joy. They step from the melancholy bedside of a dying man to the joyful bedside of a young mother, from the squalor of a tenement room to the laughter and rollicking play of a junior department picnic, from the dramatic intensity of a domestic quarrel to the routine matter-of-factness of a quarterly church business meeting.

Let the pastor meet the changing episodes of life one at a time, not waiting to live his life at some future time, but living it as he goes, and living it always at its fullest! Someone has said: "Today well lived makes every yesterday a dream of happiness and every tomorrow a vision of hope. Look well to this day."

By following such a course, John Wesley was able to live a long, busy, and fruitful life. He early learned the art of organizing his time. This was as important as his skill in organizing his followers.

"John Wesley's conversation is good," observed Samuel Johnson, "but he is never at leisure. He is always obliged to go at a certain hour." But another said of Wesley, "Although he was always in haste, he made the fine distinction of never permitting himself to be in a hurry."

There were three major interests in the life of William E. Gladstone: politics, literature, and religion. We are told that in his home there were three desks. On one were the books and papers on politics; on another were the books and manuscripts connected with his literary pursuits; on the third were the materials related to his theological studies. Thus he could move from one desk to another, leaving behind the material on one to concentrate on the material on another. For this reason, he was able in the course of his active and responsible life not only to perform exceedingly well his duties as a statesman, but also to produce such monumental works as *Homer and the Homeric Age* and *The Impregnable Rock of Scripture*. He could do all this because he had learned to organize his efforts and to isolate one activity from another.

F. B. Meyer, to whom reference already has been made, appears to have possessed this same ability. His powers of concentration were strong, and he could turn easily from one task to the next and be at his best in it. He would not permit interruptions to distract him. This is an important matter, for inevitably the minister's time will be invaded. While preparing a sermon or writing an article, he may have to answer the telephone or receive a caller. He must not fret about this. It is part of his calling, and he should never be too busy to give proper attention to those who may wish to confer with him. He must develop the ability to pass from one situation to another smoothly, and then back again. He must develop his powers of concentration.

By careful allotment of time and energy and by methodical self-discipline, the pastor can find adequate time for sermon preparation, and also for the pastoral calling and matters of church administration. Thus he can avoid the tension that comes when he is poorly prepared for his supreme responsibilities on the Lord's Day.

Alexander Maclaren, who was distinguished for his excellent sermons, realized his need for continuous study. He was convinced that many pastors took up too much of their time with details, and thus deprived themselves of the time needed for adequate study and sermon preparation.

While Maclaren was pastor at Union Chapel, he frequently was invited to preach in Manchester and in other neighboring communities. Usually he declined, saying, "My first duty is to my own congregation."

Victor Hugo wrote: "Have courage for the great sorrows of life, and patience for the small ones, and when you have laboriously accomplished your daily task, go to sleep in peace. God is awake."

It is a wise minister who learns to handle his moods, even though he may not fully understand them. Of course, to understand one's moods is to take a long step toward the successful handling of them; but it is a rare person who understands himself completely.

As has been pointed out, periods of depression come upon all of us. They are an inescapable fact of life. They are not always due to frustration or ill health. They may come in regular recurring cycles, and should not be regarded with undue concern. They may come after periods of highly accelerated activity and peaks of accomplishment, or after weeks of especially hard work and trying circumstances.

All this is to be regarded as a part of normal living. Doubt or depression, at such a time, does not necessarily signal a crisis. No one can live always on a high plane of undisturbed tranquility. After the mountaintop, the valley.

When the inevitable reaction sets in, the pastor should not be dismayed, neither should he reproach himself unduly. At such a time, however, it may be well for him to defer making decisions of major and far-reaching importance. The depressed mood will pass. It is essential that the minister learn how to handle his moods, instead of permitting his moods to handle him. He must learn how to work with himself, assured all the while of divine comfort and assistance.

It is well to remember that the assurance of the existence of God is not found through wisdom only. Although wisdom is a most valuable auxiliary in the search for God, it nevertheless is true that "the world did not know God through wisdom" (1 Cor. 1:21). The mind may find in the natural universe compelling evidences of the existence of a First Cause or of a Supreme Being, but it is in the heart of man that God makes himself fully known. It is in the human soul that God's voice is first heard. Those who seek for God through intellect only are doomed forever to doubt. They wend a circuitous way through a labyrinth of vain speculations, and at the end grope along the blank wall of spiritual frustration.

Horace Bushnell stated that as a young educator he had tried to find a religion through his intellectual efforts, only to discover that all the while he was pushing it away. "I was taken back to New Haven," he confessed, "where partly by reason of a better atmosphere in religion I was to think myself out of my overthinking and discover how far above reason is trust." Bushnell affirms that he found God through the spiritual experience of prayer.

Maude Royden relates that it was in much the same way that she found God. Her parents piously, but mistakenly, believed that her physical deformity and its attendant pain were a chastisement sent upon her by God. She says that she accepted this suggestion, but never really confronted it.

When she became a student at Oxford, all the remnants of her childhood faith disappeared with scarcely a struggle. The faith she had been taught as a child was rigid and unequal to her expanding horizon. She discarded the idea that God had sent lameness and suffering upon her. Indeed, she ceased to think of God at all.

Then she heard a sermon that made her think of Jesus as a teacher like Plato or Aristotle. She suddenly realized that she had learned more of their teachings than of his. She determined to make a thorough study of all that Jesus had said and done. The more she studied his teachings, the more she became convinced that they should be tried. She set out resolutely to put them into practice.

"The trial was a failure," she explained, "but in the failure was a mystery. The more I failed, the more profoundly conscious I became of Christ as a power. This feeling remained with me, and it grew stronger with time."

Not long after that, she met a woman who had left the Church of England and had joined the Quakers. By her she was induced to try prayer.

She continues her account in these words: "I besieged the throne of grace at a Quaker meeting, in the silence of prayer, so earnestly that I was physically exhausted. When I had no further words of entreaty, I heard a voice in my soul say, 'Yes, I have something to say to you when you stop your shouting.'

"Thus I perceived the difference between physical silence and spiritual. I began to cultivate with peace of soul the silence of the spirit which is the atmosphere of surrender, of dependence. Out of this silence came a faith against which the powers of hell could not prevail. . . . I had found the secret. I could use the power."

It is possible that one never achieves full maturity of faith unless one has first experienced the sharp probings of doubt. Doubt is the crucible in which the dross of an imperfect, immature faith is burned out, and in which only the residue of genuine worth is permitted to remain. Doubt can be a stepping-stone to faith. It can be the black chrysalis out of which a winged faith will emerge.

Doubt upsets a man's complacency and makes him examine and evaluate that which he has called faith. Through doubt man is humbled. When stripped of his own resources, he is thrown upon the resources of God. One who has not seriously doubted has not fully believed. One's faith must be tried by fire before it can be one's own. This was true of Adoniram Judson, the father of modern American missions in lands beyond the sea. With his young bride, he went to Burma. How high were their hopes! They expected to lead heathendom to the Savior; instead, heathendom brought them to a cross!

Following the death of his beloved wife, Judson underwent a period of deep anguish and depression. At thirty-eight he was burned out and work had become a grind. His associates feared that he would go insane if his mind were not diverted into other channels. But new aims and new scenes failed to interest him. In his determination to find God, he began a rigid regime of self-crucifixion, but it was all to no avail. "All this means," charged one of his associates in exasperation, "that you have been concentrating on your own body and not on the body which hung on the cross to save you from doubt." Eventually, Judson found his way through grief into a larger faith. He was able at last to say, "Drain the cup and you will find sweetness at the bottom." Thus, power came out of pain and strength out of suffering.

Trials of faith, rightly accepted and used, will serve to mellow the pastor's soul and will fashion in him a well of compassion for others. Through having suffered he will become a better preacher and a more understanding and faithful shepherd of souls.

Frederick Robertson was one of those sensitive souls who suffer much, but who through suffering come to a largeness of spirit that otherwise might not be theirs. He needed sympathy and largely was denied it, not because others were unwilling for him to have it, but because he did not know how to receive it. Without knowing it, he posted a sign which read, "No Admittance." That a man so tensely strung to self-consciousness could ever shake himself free is a noble tribute to his devotion and to that which was highest in his own soul.

"The most valuable book I possess," Robertson once averred, "is the remembrance of the trials at which I repined." Through suffering he learned to comfort those who suffered.

William Penn was expelled from Oxford because he was too religious! He could have been a seventeenth-century courtier, but he chose instead to be a seventeenth-century man of God. The world is indebted to him in that he spent more time in jails than in royal courts, in that he preached to the people instead of flattering princes, and in that he followed his conscience more than his ambition. He lived in an age that needed a conscience. Milton thundered against the times. Swift satirized them. Locke reasoned

with them. Penn became a preacher. It is significant that
he wrote his best-known book, *No Cross, No Crown,* while
he was in prison.

Penn's father, not long before his death, said to him: "I
am weary of this world. I would not live over my days
again if I could command them with a wish, for the snares
of life are greater than the snares of death. Three things
I commend to you: Let nothing in this world tempt you
to wrong your conscience. Whatever you design to do, lay
it justly and time it reasonably. Be not troubled at disappointments." This was the father who had whipped his
son and had thrown him out when he discovered he was
going to be a Quaker!

Charles Haddon Spurgeon, certainly one of the outstand-
ing pulpiteers of all times, was often seized with periods
of depression. These periods characterized him from his
boyhood. His whole life was a record of recurring physical
pain. He often had to sustain mental and spiritual effort
under protest from his inner self. "Even prayer seems like
labor," he once affirmed. Nevertheless, Spurgeon kept his
reliance on God and not on himself. "Depression comes
over me," he stated, "whenever the Lord is preparing me
for a larger blessing in my ministry."

*Let the minister think sympathetically of people, even
though they are weak, imperfect, and sinful.* However disappointed he may be, he should not become angry with
the members of his flock who yield to the temptations of
drink or infidelity. If a drunken man were to come to his
home or to his study, he should be able to put his arm
around him and to speak to him in a kindly, helpful way.
He should be able to kneel with him and to offer prayer for
him.

In short, the minister's whole life should be characterized by the mind of Christ. When Judas crept up to our Lord and placed the kiss of betrayal upon his cheek, our Lord gently entreated, "Friend, why are you here?" Alexander Maclaren called those words the last pleadings of love. A few hours later, when Jesus was upon the cross and men were shouting at him in derision, he lifted his eyes to heaven and prayed: "Father, forgive them; for they know not what they do." If the minister is to exemplify Christ, his soul must be animated by that spirit. He must not lose faith in a man, even though others may do so. He must always believe in people, in their potential goodness.

Such a spirit, fostered within, will do much to save the minister from bitterness of soul in the long pull of life, and also it will do much to save those whom he endeavors to lead.

Let the minister come to a new appreciation of the relevance of the gospel to human need, and let him concentrate on the spiritual nature of his ministry. Surely, the needs of the present hour do not differ greatly from those of the past or from those that will arise in the future. The minister, therefore, should not forget the sense of guilt that eats at many a heart; neither should he minimize the redeeming power of the One who "has borne our griefs and carried our sorrows."

Those who have made a careful study of personality and of mental health have come to appreciate the profound wisdom and insight of Jesus and of the basic pertinence of the gospel fundamentals. Man's deepest needs are spiritual, not temporal. Every problem that man encounters, in the last analysis, has spiritual import. Jesus recognized this fact. It is apparent in his dealings with such people as Nicodemus and the woman at the well in Samaria.

The necessity for the confession and forgiveness of sin, the cultivation of the sense of the Unseen Presence, the help of the Christian fellowship—these reach men where they live!

At one time William Cowper, who became noted as a writer of hymns, was committed to a mental institution for treatment. He was tormented by the conviction that he had committed sins that were unpardonable. Dr. Cotton, the superintendent of the institution, gave him a Bible to read. One day Cowper came across these words: "Whom God hath set forth to be a propitiation through faith in his blood, to declare his righteousness for the remission of sins that are past, through the forbearance of God" (Rom. 3:25, KJV).

In his *Memoirs,* Cowper writes: "Immediately I received strength to receive it. I saw the sufficiency of the atonement He had made, my pardon sealed in His blood, and all the fullness and completeness of His justification. My eyes were filled with tears, and my voice choked with transport. I could only look up to heaven, overwhelmed with love and wonder."

Are there some who are minded to quarrel with the theology implicit in that account? The fact remains that the man was helped. "It pleased God through the folly of what we preach to save those who believe" (1 Cor. 1:21).

The minister has a gospel to proclaim. Let him concentrate upon the spiritual nature of his task. Let him be assured of its primacy and urgency. If he remains true to his calling, he will always have something of superlative worth to offer. Let him not belittle it. Recognition of the relevance of the gospel affords security from doubt.

If a minister would live above doubt, let him cultivate a love of souls. "God is love, and he who abides in love abides in God, and God abides in him" (1 John 4:16).

A minister, with most of his life behind him, became a victim of doubt. During his early years he had been faithful in sounding the note of evangelism, but as the years went by his message changed and the triumphant note in it was silenced. Critical study, foreign travel, and secular interests claimed his attention. True, he was hungry for manifestations of the power of the gospel to change lives, but he did not see those manifestations and a sense of failure was reflected in his preaching. In his sermons censoriousness began to supplant love. He called it the note of prophecy, but in reality it was fault-finding born of disappointment and doubt.

"I believed in my heart that I intended only good," he said, "but it was not unpleasant to watch the arrows of sarcasm as they left the pulpit." He became unpopular and unhappy. However, as he wavered and was on the verge of forsaking his calling, he chanced to come under the influence of a congregation of vital believers. In that invigorating atmosphere, a new spiritual power entered into his soul. He became aware that it was the note of personal responsibility for those who were spiritually impoverished that had dropped out of his preaching. That congregation, with its concern for the lost, reclaimed him for kingdom usefulness.

"I began once again to pay attention to individuals," he said. "I sought to win them to Christ. . . . The pastor in me was reborn."

Another pastor made this revealing statement: "I have learned not to think of my life in terms of a job to be done, of a tangible stint of work to be accomplished, but rather to think of it as the maintaining of a certain quality of life imparted by God, as a being rather than a doing—a quality of life which proves to be actively redemptive as it flows along. The job no longer is to sit down and puzzle out what I can do to serve my fellowmen; it now is to discover God's picture for my life, and where God feels it needs to tie in with the lives of others."

The minister is not to seize a cause; the cause is to seize him. It must possess him. It must sweep him into a new course of action. It must fill his soul. That is to say, he must feel upon him the compelling hand of Jesus Christ. Then his commitment to this "cause"—which is Christ's cause—will be his armor when doubt assails him.

It was in this wise that John Wesley was sustained. He possessed a strong constitution, but it was not physical strength alone that saw him through the turbulent years of his active life. He was censured by bishops, denounced by high-church clergy, and slandered by pamphleteers, but no storm shook his soul. He said that it was his rule always to look a hostile mob squarely in the face. This he did, and he was as calm when facing a mob as when he was in his study. Tranquility in the midst of hostility came through complete devotion to a worthy cause.

Wesley regarded all the trouble that came to him as merely incidental to the great cause to which he had given himself and in which his life was to find its fulfillment. Therein was the secret of his courage and strength.

This bondage to a great and supremely worthy cause explains also the sturdiness of John Mason Peck, pioneer preacher of the Midwest and father of The American Baptist Home Mission Society.

Peck left his home in the east and journeyed to Illinois and Missouri, then frontier territory. He went there to plant the kingdom of God, a business in which the settlers who had preceded him were not interested. His center of operations was St. Louis, which has been described as "a sprawling, brawling settlement, consisting of Anglo-Americans, French, Africans, a few business and professional men, and a liberal sprinkling of scoundrels." Even the more "respectable" citizens spent much of their time drinking and gambling. In fact, there were many blasphemous infidels who made an open mockery of the Lord's Supper, and who shouted ribald prayers and hymns upon the street. They frequently boasted that the Sabbath would never cross the Mississippi.

In addition to this active opposition, Peck had to contend with the rigors of a primitive, outdoor life to which he was not accustomed, and with the indifference and the dilatoriness of the Home Mission Board. When he was almost dead with fever, he received word from the Board that it had decided to discontinue its support of his work. On top of this discouragement, three of his children died and had to be buried on the plains. The schools he had established in St. Louis and St. Charles had to be closed. Some church people, who should have been his friends, opposed him. Despite these disappointments, he struggled, prayed, and sacrificed that his great dream might come true. He had the strength to persevere, for his heart was wholly consecrated to a consuming cause; namely, the laying in that vast region of a foundation for a civilization that would be truly Christian.

The Baptist denomination, and indeed the entire Christian world, is eternally indebted to him for Shurtleff College, at Alton, Illinois, and for the noble spirit and example he left, culminating in the challenging home mission program of Baptists today.

The minister who would successfully withstand doubt must learn the priceless worth of patience. He must "learn to labor and to wait." He must be patient, for growth takes time.

It is the child who cannot wait, who demands immediate results, who must have his answer now. It is the child who begins a task with enthusiasm, then loses interest in it before it has been completed. It is the child who has a short span of attention. It is the child—and the immature adult—who is lacking in patience.

The minister labors with a mysterious, elusive substance: human life. He labors with a resistant substance: the human will. He labors with a retentive substance: the human mind.

In his work, he sows a seed whose blossom he may never live to behold. The seed must be given time to grow. All growth takes time. The seed he sows has eternity in it; it possesses a vitality all its own. The pastor's responsibility is to sow the seed faithfully. When he has done that, he has done all that he can. It is God who gives the increase. The soul cannot be forced. As the earth brings forth of itself, so also does the soul.

To some, faith is given as a flash of light; others must grope for it, or they must wait for it as men wait for the dawn. In the final analysis, faith is a gift. It is bestowed where there is patient endeavor. Faith, however, is not something to be wrested from God by the sheer force of a determined will. Faith is something that God gives to the soul that is patient, teachable, and obedient.

It may take some men a lifetime to come to full-orbed faith. Faith is like the morning. It comes slowly, and by almost imperceptible degrees. So it is with the patient, willing soul. Gradually, the shadows disappear. The soul becomes luminous, the heart is filled with harmony. Then, when faith has come, it will not be something that can be comprehended by the rational powers of the mind. It will be something that has dawned as warmly and graciously upon the soul as a summer sunrise.

5

THE PROBLEM OF GUILT

IT NOT INFREQUENTLY HAPPENS that an earnest and sincere minister becomes burdened with an intolerable sense of guilt. This guilty feeling, of course, may be due to some sin which he has sought to hide. Certainly his ministerial ordination does not exempt him from temptation; in fact, his high calling exposes him to some insidious temptations which those in less privileged positions are spared. If there has been actual wrongdoing in his life—whether a sin of commission or of omission—the minister needs to deal with the situation vigorously. He must travel the hard road of confession, repentance, and restitution wherever possible. He must seek forgiveness from those whom he has injured, and from his heavenly Father, whom he has injured most of all. Nothing written in the following paragraphs is intended to minimize the seriousness of sin or to excuse it, whether the sin be in the life of a minister or in the life of a lay person.

There are times, however, when a minister feels morally and spiritually defeated, although there has been, so far as one may judge, no gross sin in his personal life and no distressing moral defection in his conduct. In these cases the problem may best be designated as one of overconscientiousness. There are some aspects of overconscientiousness that need consideration in this connection.

Various Aspects of Overconscientiousness

By a noble and wholly commendable impulse, the minister feels impelled to be as much like his Lord as possible, both in his inner life and in his conduct before the public. This desire, of course, is wholly commendable. But in his conduct there is bound to be a disparity between the ideal and the actual. An extreme sensitivity with respect to personal conduct, inner attitudes, and fidelity to his pastoral responsibilities may induce in the minister an acute sense of failure. He may conclude that he is not good enough in his life—his thoughts, motivations, and actions—to be a minister of the gospel. In such cases, it may be merely that the minister is trying too hard.

Perhaps the most enervating results of such overconscientiousness occur when the minister feels that his motivation is not what it should be. Whereas he knows that he should be actuated by an altruistic, unselfish spirit, he may discern within himself motives which are inimical to that kind of living. If self-concern looms large in his thinking, he recognizes himself as still a selfish person and is oppressed with a sense of shame. His desire is to be actuated by kind intentions, loving thoughts, and forgiving attitudes, but there are times when he is torn by tempests of envy and anger. These periods astonish him and crush him. In consequence, he severely rebukes himself for his unbridled conduct.

He wishes to mature in the spirit of tolerance, forgiveness and magnanimity, and he is displeased with himself when he perceives that actually he has taken an ill-concealed delight in intolerance, in bigotry, or in yielding his heart to an unbecoming grudge.

He would be free from the tyranny of the love of money, and is profoundly ashamed when he confronts himself with evidences of his deep-seated covetousness.

He wishes to be spiritual and to despise the sensual, but he may discover to his dismay that there is deep within him that which takes furtive pleasure in sensuality. He finds himself surreptitiously contemplating with guilty pleasure the attractions of license and released passion.

He would emulate the spirit of Jesus by displaying a true humility, and he hardly knows what to do with the vagrant emotions of pride that swell within him, whenever some new public recognition or unusual honor comes his way.

The minister may recognize all of these unworthy emotions and acknowledge their incongruity with his calling. At the same time, he may sense in his soul a fundamental identification with them. This identification will perplex and dismay him. Thereupon, realizing that these baser feelings should have no place in a Christian's life, he may fall into the error of flogging himself. Flagellation is not an uncommon phenomenon. It arises from something quite fundamental in human nature, whenever one aspires to the higher life. Whereas the Flagellants have wielded leather lashes to keep their bodies under, the pastor who suffers from such a sense of guilt wields the invisible whips of self-reproach and self-castigation. The only difference is that the invisible whips cut more deeply and lastingly.

A second aspect of overconscientiousness comes into view when a minister is seriously disturbed by a recollection of misconduct indulged in by him in his early life, and of which he now is heartily ashamed. These misdemeanors may not have been gross deviations from the accepted norm of deportment, but he looks upon them as infractions of the moral code. He feels that they reflect on his integrity, his trustworthiness, or his good judgment.

Perhaps he remembers with undying chagrin an unpremeditated, indiscreet, and damaging remark. He earnestly wishes he might be able to recall it, but he realizes how impossible it is to expunge the harm done by it to others and also to himself. With all his heart, he wishes he might live over again those few minutes.

Perhaps he remembers with humiliation the ridiculous spectacle he made of himself when he became overcome by anger. He wishes that he might retrace his steps. If he had it to do over again, he would not be so foolish.

Perhaps he recollects a day when in planning his career he made an unwise choice, took the wrong turn in the road. The memory of this mistake may disturb his slumbers, may reproach him, to such an extent that he comes to feel that he is one of the most foolish of men, and that, as a minister, he is unworthy of the confidence of trustful church workers, good women, and little children.

Be assured that these are not idle observations. They represent poignant reality. More than one minister, in a moment of extreme temptation, has yielded to sin. Thereafter, he feels his degradation so keenly that he can never forgive himself. How humiliating such memories can be is revealed in the case of Paul, who cried: "I am unfit . . . to be called an apostle, because I persecuted the church of God" (1 Cor. 15:9). Paul never succeeded in banishing from his mind the memory of the havoc and slaughter which he had wrought upon the followers of Jesus. However, he sought to forget the past in order that he might devote his full strength to right living in the present.

There is yet another area in which a conscientious pastor may feel that he has fallen short; namely, in the performance of his pastoral duties.

As a minister, he wishes to do his full duty; he wants to give of himself all that there is to give. But regardless of his best efforts and of his self-emptying, he always sees ahead of him many more duties equally pressing. The thought of the "something more" that needs to be done gives him no rest.

He cannot relax, for he knows that there are aged, lonely, and distressed people in the community. He cannot be at peace with himself, for he knows that there are those in hospitals who suffer and need him at their bedsides. He cannot delay, for he knows that there are homes which are threatened with collapse. He knows that there are spiritual wanderers who need a shepherd and a flock.

The conscientious minister feels that he cannot be lenient with himself when in the presence of need or distress. He taxes his strength to the utmost in his effort to respond to all of the calls. He rises early to pore over his books and to prepare his sermons. He labors late and long with delicate, time-consuming problems involving church organization and personnel. These matters require great tact and make heavy demands upon his spiritual resources.

In the evening he cannot sit quietly at home, even for an hour, to relax with his family. He is transfixed with the thought, "How can I enjoy myself and be at ease when there is so much to be done?" This awareness of unfinished work pursues him even when he tries to take a vacation. He reproaches himself that he is not at his post. He is not on call for duty. It is not enough that he should try to shoulder all the responsibilities of his parish while he is in it; he must try to manage it and serve it by remote control while he is absent.

Unfortunately, the minister who has such feelings is usually the last person who has real reason to have them. The pastor who does not experience such feelings probably is the one who would do well to experience them, at least to a healthy extent. For there are those who unwittingly lapse into laziness and evasion, a state which often is misnamed busyness or overwork.

Furthermore, when the minister has done his best to save the home threatened with dissolution or to reclaim the wanderer, and has met with only limited success or none at all, he is likely to become burdened with a feeling of failure. The effect of this will be felt in the family situation. Harried by his determination to measure up to the highest demands of the ministry, he spends all of his time in behalf of his congregation and has nothing left for his family. Those whom he loves best receive from him only fragments of attention and outbursts which are due to spent nerves.

There is much truth as well as pathos in the following story. Like many another pastor, this man was at his work early every morning and did not return to his home until late at night. His little daughter, of course, was in bed when he left and in bed again when he returned. One night, on returning to his home, he found a note pinned to his pillow. It was written in his daughter's childish hand and read: "I would like to have a conference with my pastor when he comes in." That strikes a tender chord in all of us.

Such a minister, already feeling a sense of failure in the performance of his ministerial duties, now has the added realization that he has neglected his family. He is aware that his little brood is growing up, that soon they will have flown from the paternal nest. Yet he has scarcely come to know them. He has not concerned himself sufficiently with their growth and character development. He feels that he has failed also as a parent.

Even as he comes to this realization, there occurs the board meeting, the committee session, the luncheon club, or the visitation campaign. Whatever it may be, it says: "Leave your family. Be on your way. This is your bounden duty." The resultant tension produces irritability. He repulses the demands which his wife and children make upon him for time and attention. He rejects them gruffly, then pays the penalty in terms of regret.

The problem here is of more importance than one may at first realize. In the home, many life-or-death battles are fought out. A man rises or falls in accordance with the atmosphere of the home. He needs the understanding and support which his wife can give him. If he has it, he can surmount almost any obstacle. But he cannot expect to have this understanding and support if he neglects his home and family.

A Right Attitude Toward Our Human Limitations

In those cases where the minister suffers from a sense of guilt which rises, not so much from actual sin as from over-conscientiousness, possibly his greatest need is to gain a right attitude toward his human limitations.

The minister needs to acquire what may be termed "courage despite imperfection." At first, this may seem to be a misstatement. One may have assumed that the element most necessary to successful living is "courage based on perfection." The drive toward perfection is commendable and arouses admiration. But whereas such a drive has its virtues, it has also its flaws. One can never achieve perfection. Perfection is not an attribute of man, but an attribute of deity.

All of us can become much better than we are, but none of us can become perfect. What we need is the courage to keep on trying, despite the realization that there will always be some imperfection in our lives. The minister must have the will to keep on ministering to the erring, even though he does not succeed in bringing back a single sinner from the error of his way. He must have a mind to press toward the mark in personal righteousness, even though he may continually stumble and fall. He must accept the inevitable shortcomings in his work, not that he may become complacent with respect to them, but that he may become less discouraged by them.

The minister had best accept his essential humanity and then cease to worry about it. If he permits the whole of his attention to be taken up by the imperfections in his character, he will surely be defeated. When one is learning to ride a bicycle, one discovers that to concentrate on missing a bump ahead usually means to hit it. Let the overly conscientious minister, therefore, concentrate on the open road rather than the bumps, and let him not be unduly dismayed if a spill occasionally occurs.

It is never possible to erase tension completely from one's mind. Indeed, a certain amount of tension is necessary to a well-tuned life. Without tension, one would never approach his best; there would be no incentive to progress. But too much tension is as dangerous and sinful as complacency.

The minister should be able to distinguish within himself that which can be changed and that which cannot be changed. He should be ready to modify whatever needs to be modified and to accept whatever cannot be modified. He must learn to take himself in hand, and to deal with himself with a mature wisdom and patience.

The son of a minister felt called of God to follow in his father's vocation. He graduated from the seminary with an excellent record. The future held for him a bright prospect. Upon reaching his first charge, a small parish, he threw himself unreservedly into the life and work of the ministry. He gave body, mind, heart, and soul to his calling. Then, suddenly, he abandoned it all. "I'm not good enough to be a minister," he explained. "I don't deserve all that has been done for me."

A survey of the situation revealed that the early religious influences which had been thrown about him had been strict, stern, and authoritarian. He had been made to feel that being a Christian was a very difficult matter, that one had to try very hard if one were to be worthy of the name. For one thing, one had to observe all the biblical commandments. The result was that he had set before himself a pattern of perfection. This standard of conduct was so exacting and so impossible of attainment that it wrecked his initial attempt at being a pastor.

When the perfectionist pattern by which this young minister had sought to live was challenged by the realities of life, it proved unattainable. If, now, he can be given a new outlook on life, if he can be re-educated, his effectiveness can be saved. But before he can recover from so harmful an attitude, the very foundations of his life and his habits of thought must be shaken.

Beauty of character, after all, is not achieved by trying hard. It does not come through conscious effort, but, like faith, is a gift from God. It is a quality of life that is fashioned within us, without our knowledge, when we commit ourselves completely to God. In Memorial Chapel at Harvard University, there is a tablet honoring Dr. Francis Peabody, the venerable educator. It reads: "His precept was glorified by his example while for thirty-three years he moved among the teachers and students of Harvard College, and wist not that his face shone."

This is reminiscent of the ageless story of *The Great Stone Face,* a story more familiar to earlier generations than to our own. In it, we learn that the prophecy current in the valley found its fulfillment in the person of Ernest, one who had not anticipated anything of the sort. Unknown to Ernest, the grandeur, magnanimity, and wisdom with which his imagination had hallowed the distant granite profile had entered into his soul through a profound process of personal identification. Without his being aware of it, he became more and more that which he believed the face to represent.

The minister needs the courage to press on in spite of shortcomings in personality, motivation, and deed. He must not permit himself to be delayed, sidetracked, or overcome by a striving after an unattainable goal, a goal that serves only to sharpen the conflict in his soul.

The attainments of life are an "in-spite-of" process. One becomes happy in spite of trouble. One grows to emotional maturity in spite of pain. It is also true that life is a "because-of" process. One becomes happy because of trouble. One becomes emotionally mature because of pain. A certain amount of adversity is necessary to strengthen and sharpen one's latent powers. The faithful minister, therefore, will not be deterred by his shortcomings. He will not permit them to turn him aside from his calling. Instead, he will seek to turn his imperfections into assets. Only so will his life become the blessing to mankind that it was meant to be.

Certainly, the minister must not flog himself because of his imperfections, real or fancied. There is point, therefore, in the humorous story of the minister who asked the bride if she took this man "for better or for worse." "He can't be no worse," she replied, "and there ain't no chance of his bein' any better, so I just takes him as is." Any minister could be far worse, and it is equally clear that he could be far better, but to be so he must first take himself as he is. He must understand that if he yields himself to God, God can use him, in spite of his limitations.

John B. Gough was a truly great man, but what strange and baffling contradictions stirred within him! As a temperance lecturer, he could move thousands to the depths of their being and inspire them to abandon their drinking. Yet, for some years, he was himself a victim of the evil he denounced. A few hours after a particularly inspiring lecture he might be found in an intoxicated condition, incapable of coherent conversation. Then, for days, he would wallow in the slough of despair and self-contempt. However, he had a faithful friend, one who never forsook him. That friend was Lyman Beecher. He would seek out Gough, put his arm around him, speak kindly to him, and urge him to get up and try again. At last, Gough, by his public confessions and great sincerity, established himself in the confidence of his hearers, and his reputation as a lecturer steadily increased.

Peter was so sure of himself! And then so chagrined when he discovered how weak he actually was! He felt that there was nothing left for him to do but to give up and run away. The Fourth Gospel, however, beautifully narrates Peter's restoration. Eventually he was able to say, "We must obey God rather than men" (Acts 5:29).

Despite our obvious imperfections we must press on, realizing that God repeatedly has used imperfect instruments to bless the world. Out of weakness, he calls forth strength. Paul, the apostle, certainly found this to be true.

The minister must master the exacting art of self-discipline. This has been said in another connection, but in a day when the necessity for self-control is sometimes questioned, it needs to be said again. The minister, so far as in him lies, must manage his emotions. It is by so doing that he achieves maturity.

Sometimes a part of the minister's difficulty grows out of the fact that he permits ideas to become tools to him, instead of becoming disciplines by which to live. He is constantly looking for sermonic material, and when good ideas come his way he is likely to think of them in relation to his congregation, instead of in relation to his own life.

A young preacher, having read an article dealing with some personality problems which ministers need to solve, exclaimed, "Say, that's good material for a sermon!" The articles had been written for ministers—for *him!* But he thought first of a sermon to others!

"The kingdom of heaven," said Jesus, "is like leaven which a woman took and hid in three measures of meal, till it was all leavened" (Matt. 13:33). However, the hiding process involved kneading and blending the yeast with the meal. This called for effort.

Addressing some Yale ministerial students on the art of preaching, Phillips Brooks said: "It cannot be the mere training in certain tricks, or even the furnishing with abundant knowledge. It must be nothing less than the kneading and tempering of a man's whole nature till it becomes of such consistency and quality as to be capable of transmission."

The minister will do well to remember that which he is fond of telling others; namely, that he does not walk alone. An Unseen Companion is always at his side.

A student once asked Dr. Brooks if conscious personal fellowship with Jesus Christ was a part of Christianity. The great preacher was silent for a moment, and then replied with impressive earnestness: "Conscious personal fellowship with Jesus Christ *is* Christianity." No minister can rise to heights of spiritual influence unless he finds and practices the presence of God.

How discordant our lives! But when the Master lends his hand, and his strong, skillful fingers begin to move along the keyboard of our days, a miracle happens. The discords change to harmony. The faltering notes are caught up and mingled with a mighty chord we thought we had lost forever. "Where sin increased, grace abounded all the more" (Rom. 5:20).

Confession and the Divine Forgiveness

In what has been stated—let it be repeated—there has been no thought of minimizing the seriousness of actual misconduct. Indeed, sin, wherever it exists, exacts its due penalty. *If a minister has surrendered to sin, he will know no peace of mind until he has sought and received the divine forgiveness.*

If a minister has been guilty of gross misconduct, the consequent disturbance of conscience may reveal itself in impaired health, in a confession of atheism, or in a holier-than-thou attitude.

If a minister, through being busy with other things, has neglected his pulpit preparation or his pastoral duties, the resultant inner disquietude may manifest itself in a nagging sense of failure.

If a minister has been guilty of pose and hypocrisy and has neglected to keep his own life spiritually adequate, or if he has become filled with pride and self-seeking and has lost the shepherd heart, then the inevitable self-contempt may display itself in spiritual dry rot. Self-rejection, cynicism, boredom, and censoriousness are among the penalties paid by ministers who have ceased to be faithful. Paul was not speaking idle words when he counseled, "Do not neglect the gift you have" (1 Tim. 4:14).

The minister who is burdened in any of the ways which have been mentioned will know no peace of mind until he comes to personal integrity. This is the only true peace. He must frankly acknowledge his sin. This is not easy, for the truth about oneself may be disagreeable; but it must be faced. The confession of sin is much more than a sanctimonious gesture. It is fundamental to satisfactory living. The minister must face himself before he can face his God.

Such a minister needs to discard his easy tolerance and comfortable self-indulgence and actually surrender his life to God. Let him give himself to God and once again become a shepherd of souls. He will be astonished at the peace and power that will then come to him.

Jesus did not demand of Peter that he be perfect or even brilliant. He merely bade him feed his sheep. It was by so doing that Peter would show his love. But before Peter could come into the possession of spiritual power he had first to acknowledge his weakness. Something humiliating and humbling had to happen to him. He had to confess his sin in order that he might become free of it. Out of that painful experience emerged a new and vastly stronger Peter, who was a mighty comfort to the little band of first-century believers.

A pastor had ceased to pray, because (so he said) he saw no real benefit from it. To all outward appearances, his work seemed highly successful. He had built a new church, but he realized that he had done it in his own strength. All the praise that had come to him had served only to increase his sense of guilt. He could not avoid the self-accusation that during the two years of his pastorate he had failed miserably in his essential ministry.

"I knew what pastors were expected to do," he confessed, "and I had not done it. I had not changed a single life."

The frankness of two other pastors (they had spoken in a meeting where honest confessions were being made) was a severe blow to his pride. He determined to surrender his life anew to Jesus Christ. With that in mind, he sought a conference with an older, understanding pastor. In the course of their discussion he confessed to a number of old-fashioned sins which had been hindering his communion with God.

In relating his experience, he said: "I prayed, and in my prayer I made a definite and complete surrender. Immediately there came a feeling of release and peace. It was a matter of surrendering new areas of conduct and attitude successively, for I realized that I had been holding out on God. By this means, guidance became more real, and I felt the power of God's Holy Spirit increasingly taking possession of me."

Another youthful minister confessed that he first learned this secret when he came into the intimate presence of men who had a quality of life which he lacked. He found that they possessed their spiritual power because they had been willing to pay the price of it.

He saw that he had been bound by fear. He had been afraid that he would lose his place. He had a desire to write, but it was not for the glory of God; it was for his own personal advancement. He was afraid that if he permitted anything that resembled an emotional display he might lose an esteemed reputation for scholarship. He was afraid that he might forfeit his intellectual integrity if he were to submit to the will of God and try to live by divine guidance. He was afraid he might lose his sense of humor if he were to permit himself to dwell too much upon the sacred character of his calling. He was afraid of losing his friends if he were to take too firm a stand for his religious convictions. However, when he had seen all this, he so desired the peace that genuine integrity imparts that he resolutely cast his fears aside. He honestly confessed his self-centeredness and experienced indescribable relief.

A cynical clergyman once explained: "I'm fed up with this business of religion! I'm sorry, but I can't help it." But when this clergyman finally summoned the courage to compare his life with the life of a truly surrendered Christian, he confessed: "I saw for the first time my shameful self-love; I saw it in startling contrast to the marvelous self-giving love of Christ. On my knees I surrendered everything to God—and I meant it! From that day my life was different."

An elderly minister attended a meeting of earnest pastors who were seeking greater spiritual power. His was a sorry story of failure and unhappiness. He revealed to his brethren the torment resulting from the state of compromise in which he had been living. Because he was officially committed to it, he was trying to proclaim a victorious message; but in his private life he was utterly defeated.

"What is the way out?" he queried. "I've been preaching a gospel I would believe to be true, but which, so far, I've not been able to verify in my own experience." In the course of an intimate interview, he came to see that he must, once and for all, discard all his self-indulgence. He decided to live the transparent, sharing life. In so doing, he came to experience the truth of what he had been preaching.

If the pastor is to be at peace with himself, his life must be of such a quality that it will bear examination.

One sometimes finds ministers who have gone far enough in their faith to be melancholy, but not far enough to be glad. Consider the confession of another pastor: "I saw that without adequate discipline my life would never be one hundred per cent effective. Through careful, sustained meditation I faced up to the fourfold challenge of honesty, purity, unselfishness, and love. I saw four things that had to be put right in my life. I had not forgiven a certain person who had wronged me. There was a restitution I had not made. There were dubious pleasures I had not been willing to give up. There was a sin of long standing I had not confessed. With these things straightened out, I came into release and new power. For the first time, I began to get daily guidance from God. I knew I could rely on it, because my own life was now disciplined. I entered into a period of radiant joy." Another pastor, having had a taste of the new inner dynamic, lapsed into his old ways. He forsook the ideal of bringing people to Christ and gave all his effort to building up the organization of his church. He polished his sermons until they shone, but he neglected individuals except as he might encounter them in occasional calling. The major obstructions that kept him from spiritual release and power were not gross sins. They were the insidious sins of ambition and pride.

So long as a minister is preoccupied with his own problems, antipathies, and moods, he will do those things which he thinks are necessary to compensate for his inferiorities and maladjustments. When, however, he surrenders to God, the whole tenor of his living changes. He no longer regards himself as the emotional center of all things. He no longer is so sensitive to slights, real or imagined. Instead, he becomes engrossed in his true calling of rebuilding lives, and straightway begins to live more adequately.

The minister, therefore, will do well to question himself honestly about his professional ambition, about his moods of discouragement, about his self-pity, about his grudges against persons in authority. He will do well to examine his disposition at home, his mental laziness, his intemperance, his sins of the flesh and of the mind, his tendency to be careless in his preaching, his lack of prayer and Bible study, his favoritism, and his censorious spirit. He may need to seek out some fearless, forthright soul who, like the prophet Nathan, will speak the truth to him and help him to make a clean breast of the true state of affairs.

He must permit the center of his life to be filled with the Holy Spirit.

6

THE PROBLEM OF CONCEIT

PAINTED UPON THE CEILING of the Sistine Chapel in Rome is a mighty panorama showing in dramatic sequence the creation of the world, the fall of man, and the deluge. These majestic scenes constitute what is considered to be the greatest single work from the mind and hand of Michelangelo. In this heroic-sized painting there is a representation of the Creator, who is shown in the act of creating Adam. A close examination of the representation of God reveals an interesting fact. The face of God bears a striking resemblance to that of the artist!

Comparing the face of God, as painted there, with the extant portraits of Michelangelo, we see that the lines on the two faces are similar. So also are the furrows between the eyebrows. The molding of the nose is much the same in both. The lips have the same breadth and sternness. The faces of both are full of something enigmatic and inscrutable.

Indeed, it appears that Michelangelo, whether by accident or by design, painted God in his own image!

That a man should liken himself to God is not an isolated phenomenon. It was not an uncommon occurrence in that day; it is not uncommon in this day. Many persons come to think of themselves as God. Consciously or unconsciously they become afflicted with what may be termed the God-complex.

Pride, of course, is universal. One can never be completely free of it. As a matter of fact, a certain measure of pride is both normal and healthy. It furnishes the individual with an incentive for perseverance and greater achievement. Pride does not become detrimental unless it gets out of hand and eventuates in a distorted inordinate self-esteem.

Similarly, when a proper self-respect turns into conceit and dominates the whole personality, it becomes abnormal. It then is dangerous to the individual himself, and dangerous, as well as obnoxious, to others also. Such conceit is wholly false. It may be merely a substitute for one's failure to achieve self-confidence and self-respect in a legitimate way.

Certain aspects of this overweening conceit call for closer consideration. One of these aspects rests upon the myth of a superior endowment.

Consider such a case as this. A young minister, with a humble background, meets with a considerable measure of success in a small parish. He attracts some attention. Soon he is promoted (if the term may be properly used in this connection) to a larger and more influential parish. His talents, although to his credit, are not eminently superior. His elevation, however, leads him to think that they are exceptional. Believing himself possessed of superior ability, he becomes puffed up. His manner in the pulpit becomes pompous. His speech becomes ponderous. He gives the impression that his words, however inconsequential, are pearls of wisdom. He assumes the dignity which he thinks is commensurate with his elevated position.

To such a man the sweetest music is the sound of his own voice. He is transfixed by admiration of his superior intellect. He feels confident that he can discern and understand the motives of others. He stands ready to speak as an authority on any subject. The only correct analysis of any problem, he feels sure, is his analysis. These qualities, however, are not those which characterize the really great; instead, they are the character qualities of the "would be" great.

It is said that the late Dr. William Temple, Archbishop of Canterbury, was impatient with all forms of snobbery and pride, and that he possessed rare wit in squelching such pretensions.

One day a caller was ushered into his study.

"Take a chair, Mr. Jones," said Dr. Temple.

"If you please, your Grace," responded the man, "Mr. Montague-Jones."

"Oh," said Dr. Temple, "in that case, take two chairs."

The lives of truly great people, without exception, are characterized by humility and simplicity. However high their station, they feel no compulsion to appear great. Indeed, elevation is one of the surest tests of character. It has been said that if you would discover a man's true character, you need only to give him power. How he uses that power will show what sort of man he is.

This unbecoming and unwarranted conceit may be related also to the myth of superior righteousness. Where there is this belief in one's superior righteousness, it expresses itself in denunciation and despotism. It has bedeviled the Christian churches from the earliest times.

The minister, by the very nature of his calling, is peculiarly exposed to temptations of this sort. To those about him, he stands as a symbol of God. The deference with which people regard him ranges from sincere respect to adulation. In accepting their praise, often extravagant, he very easily may come to believe himself possessed, in some degree, of divine attributes.

The workings of such a warped and mistaken belief may be seen in the bloody purges of the Inquisition. In those days, mortal men presumed to sit in spiritual judgment on other mortals respecting the manner of their faith and forms of worship. The Inquisitors usurped yet another of God's prerogatives. They not only presumed to sit in judgment on others, but they also asserted the right to take the lives of those who came under their condemnation.

The crucifixion of Jesus, brought about by the consuming hatred of the ecclesiastical leaders, affords an even more appalling example. The members of the Sanhedrin, in their own minds, had identified themselves with God, and they were exercising prerogatives which belonged only to God.

The myth of superior righteousness may explain in part the enigma of John Calvin. A recent biographical work states that power flowed through his brain like wine. Intoxicated by a belief in his superior righteousness, he compelled every citizen of Geneva to profess on oath the Protestant faith.

It is said that Calvin would not tolerate showy dress, and that he sent inspectors from house to house to see that his orders were being obeyed. He punished with severity even trifling misdemeanors. He ordered three men to be imprisoned for laughing during one of his sermons. He scathingly denounced another man for asserting that he preferred to hear other preachers. As a final ignominious crown to his spurious assumptions, he commanded that Servetus, the physician, be burned at the stake for adhering to principles contrary to Protestantism.

This is not to imply that the minister should be devoid of convictions. On the contrary, there are things in which he should believe; there are things for which he should stand. Otherwise, he does violence to the integrity of his soul. However, he is to regard sin as an act against God rather than against himself. He is to move against sin, as distinguished from the sinner. He is to hate the iniquity which men do, but in his heart he is to love the wrongdoer and seek to restore him to righteousness.

Closely related to the myth of superior endowment and the myth of superior righteousness is the equally misleading myth of superior wisdom. A minister may convince himself that he possesses that infallible wisdom which only God possesses, and so believing he may assume responsibility for the lives and fortunes of others. It is his covert wish so to manipulate people that they will live their lives according to his ideas of what is good for them. He experiences exquisite pleasure when he sees them doing this, for he then feels a sense of power. He boils with indignation, however, when he perceives conduct contrary to his expressed wishes. His sense of importance has been offended; his words have been shown to be ineffectual.

The indignation which he then feels does not actually stem, as he would like to believe, from a sense of righteousness which has been circumvented, but from the fact that the myth of his superior wisdom has been called in question. In other words, the minister who is afflicted in any measure with the God-complex looks upon himself as being judge, jury, and executioner all combined in one. We are solemnly warned against this ever-present danger by our Lord, who bade us cease passing judgment upon others and give thought rather to improving our own conduct.

Some biographers have stated that Dr. W. E. Orchard, the minister of King's Weigh House Church, London, may have fallen into this error. He has been described as a fighter rather than a teacher. Indeed, a question has been raised as to whether he could ever have been happy in a world which offered to him no opportunity for punching heads.

Whereas Dr. Orchard's manner was irritating to others, his opinions were sweepingly satisfactory to himself. He ridiculed those who differed with him. Sometimes, instead of discussing an issue, he would browbeat his opponents. His heart seems to have entertained little warmth and mellowness. When he complained that people did not know what Christianity is, there were some who wondered if his own definition was adequate. How much truth there may have been in these charges, we cannot say. At least, they serve to point up a temptation to which all too many eminent men succumb.

Various Expressions of the God-Complex

As has been stated above, a minister who feels thus sure of himself enjoys influencing people because of the satisfaction which it gives his ego. He may tell himself that what he does, he does only for their own good; he may feel that he is, in reality, deeply concerned for their spiritual welfare. At this point, we need to guard against making any sweeping, indiscriminate charges. The concern which ministers feel for others usually is nobly motivated. But it must be admitted that occasionally a counterfeit motivation is encountered.

Sometimes the minister's concern is not limited to a few individuals, but is so broadened in scope as to embrace the world scene. The minister may assume responsibility for the whole world.

When this occurs the minister assumes a melancholy air. He becomes burdened with care. His manner implies that he is carrying upon his frail shoulders the sins of all the world, and that he is prepared to endure the impending judgment which rightly should fall on those whom he is befriending. Such a minister is taking himself far too seriously.

The minister with the God-complex feels that he must save the world. He believes that all depends on him.

He fits very well Gamaliel Bradford's description of one phase of the many-sided personality of Theodore Roosevelt: "He forced enjoyment with the desperate, instinctive appreciation that if he let the pretense [of his own enjoyment] drop for a moment, the whole scheme of things would vanish away."

A minister who is thus burdened may protest his faith in God, but by his anxiety he denies God. He is not depending on God, though he might be the last to admit it. He has no God, because having accepted responsibility for the course of affairs, he has to that extent made himself God. He thenceforth is actuated by fear, rather than by faith.

If he had a God, he could relax. He could commit the world's destiny to God, in the assurance that after he had done his best, divine Providence would care for the rest.

It is ludicrous—when one thinks about it—that a man should become so involved with his own emotions that he can no longer think with objectivity and discernment. He cannot see how incongruous is the role which he has assumed.

There is much to be learned from the experience of the prophet Elijah. After the arduous test on Mt. Carmel was ended and when Jezebel was hot on his trail, Elijah slumped down under a juniper tree and moaned, "It is enough; now, O Lord, take away my life; for I am no better than my fathers." Later, the prophet lamented, "I, even I only, am left; and they seek my life, to take it away." It is possible that there was an indulgent smile on the face of God as he replied, "Yet I will leave seven thousand in Israel, all the knees that have not bowed to Baal" (1 Kings 19:4, 14, 18).

The assumption of infinite wisdom operates not only in the minister's relationship toward others, but also in relationship to his own inner life. In addition to feeling responsible for the conduct of others, he feels responsible for every phase of his own life.

He is accountable, of course, for his actions, his deeds and his misdeeds. But he is not accountable for the outcome of his efforts. Believing himself to be personally and completely responsible for the fruition of all his efforts, he pushes himself relentlessly toward self-realization. His lips protest faith in God, but his tense anxiety reveals that he has faith only in himself. He has usurped God's place in his life!

This is one of the most insidious aspects of disbelief. Disbelief is a very deceptive state of mind, and one who considers himself free of it may very well possess it. The mind has almost limitless powers of self-deception, and a state of anxiety may indicate an absence of any real faith in anything or in any person other than oneself.

The God-complex, therefore, is disturbing rather than satisfying; and if one's faith in one's omniscience is ever seriously disturbed (as it certainly will be), emotional consternation is the result.

The operation of the God-complex may be seen at work in the life of Saul of Tarsus, the ardent Pharisee. We find him sitting in judgment upon others. We find him driving himself remorselessly in his zeal to execute the divine wrath upon them. We find him breathing out "threatening and slaughter."

One sees in Saul a fierce demand for conformity to his ideas. Later, when as a result of his meeting with Christ he had become Paul the apostle, he said: "I myself was convinced that I ought to do many things in opposing the name of Jesus of Nazareth" (Acts 26:9). By that time, he was prepared to admit that all such strivings had proved loss.

In the days when he was persecuting the followers of Christ, we see nothing of the calm faith that characterized his later life. As a Pharisee, he felt that everything depended on him. He labored frantically, and to no avail. Later, when he had come to know Christ, he labored no less devotedly, but there was within him a calm and enabling faith. He said: "I can do all things in him who strengthens me" (Phil. 4:13).

The Origin of These Feelings

These assumptions of divine wisdom, these usurpations of divine prerogatives, may have had their origin in some severe inner conflict. Paul has given an account of the struggle he felt within himself. He lamented the fact that he had done what he wished he had not done, and that he had left undone what he wished he had done. And from the depths of his emotional and spiritual anguish he cried out: "Wretched man that I am! Who will deliver me from this body of death?" (Rom. 7:24). Undoubtedly this inner turmoil and indecision was a dominant factor in his fanatical persecution of the Christians. Traces of it lingered long after his conversion. The conflict was finally resolved by his complete identification of his will with Christ's will, but such identification and unity was not achieved at once.

Usually the minister who is constantly involved in a warfare of some sort is a man who harbors a war within himself. He has a civil war going on in his own soul.

A survey of the life of Bishop Gore of England is illuminating. There were those who thought that his countenance was not that of a man at peace with himself. If peace was there, it was an uneasy, uncertain peace. He gave the impression of being one whose soul was under a cloud.

For this reason his presence imparted no feeling of warmth or radiance. He had the aspect of a man who had conquered, but at a heavy price. He frequently declared that a man must be strong at the center of his being, if he is to be strong at the circumference. But it is possible that his strength was not that of the whole man, but only of his will. Perhaps it was a forced strength into which his affections had not wholeheartedly entered.

He held that one becomes a Christian only through a tremendous act of choice. He pressed the severity of the claims of Christ. His religion was a stern and rigid one. As he saw it, it was very hard to be a good Christian. Very little of the love of God was discernible in his spirit, because the God he preached was not pre-eminently a God of love.

When he was Canon of Westminster, he attracted a large following by his simplicity, honesty, and rectitude. When he became a bishop, these saintly qualities disappeared. The real man came to the surface. He became dogmatic. He demanded complete and literal acceptance of the creeds. He believed that Christianity would perish if there was the least wavering of belief with respect to the miraculous. He set himself up, not so much as an exponent of the faith, as the exponent of a particular view of the faith.[1]

This, conceivably, was the case also with the uncompromising Savonarola of Florence. This melancholy, austere man rose to such power that he could defy the Medici, but wherever he went he generated factions. One is moved to wonder if there may not have been some strife within Savonarola himself, some inner strife that led to the fomenting of strife without.

In other cases, this dogmatic and authoritarian attitude may have had its origin in a sense of deficiency.

One finds a strange mingling of elements in a personality of this type. Authoritarianism is mingled with questionable conduct, rigidity with instability, courage with despair. These elements create a contradiction within. They are a part of that moral imperfection and personality deficiency which set the struggle in motion. There is in such an individual a morose striving for perfection, in the face of acute despair over sinfulness. Such a person may assume the authoritarian role to compensate for the realization of his moral deficiency and to ease the goading of conscience.

Such a role is often, though not necessarily, associated with emotional instability. It is as if the individual, being

[1] The facts here given concerning Bishop Gore are drawn from *Painted Windows*, by "A Gentleman with a Duster," pseudonym of Harold Begbie. Chap. 1. Published by Mills & Boon, Limited. London, 1922.

uncertain of himself, must seize that which is unrelenting, uncompromising, and unbending—all that he is not—to appease the complaints of his offended conscience.

There are those who insist upon doctrinal purity and theological integrity because they do not possess within themselves the requisite moral purity and spiritual integrity. It is easier to be correct in dogma than in manner of life! Violent insistence on the former may be merely an effort to draw attention away from the latter.

The Treatment of These Feelings

To analyze this complex, admittedly, is easier than to prescribe a remedy. Normally—so one would suppose—a knowledge of the existence of such an emotional pattern would be sufficient to dissipate it. This would indeed be the case, but for the fact that the mind possesses almost limitless powers of self-deception. "All the ways of a man are pure in his own eyes" (Prov. 16:2). This is as true of clergymen as of all others.

It is pathetic that a man cannot see himself as others see him, but such is the case. For example, it is extremely difficult for a conceited person to realize that he is conceited. We hide ourselves from ourselves by donning various disguises. We vehemently deny, both to ourselves and to others, that we possess any uncomplimentary characteristics. Then we attribute to others the traits which we are ashamed to confess in ourselves, such as conceit, selfishness, and bad temper.

Perhaps our greatest need is some stern and abrupt reversal which will bring us to our senses.

It is only in this fashion that some will ever come to see themselves as they really are. For that reason, probably, every minister should pray for some adversity, and not complain too much if his prayer is answered. Some rude interruption may stab him wide awake and save him from becoming complacent and conceited.

The prelude to greatness is humility. True greatness consists of largeness of soul and breadth of compassion. These qualities come only to those who possess that humility which is born out of adversity.

Humility, therefore, is not synonymous with self-abnegation, and it does not imply self-abasement. It leaves room for a proper self-respect.

True humility calls for sobriety in self-appraisal. Paul's admonition is: "For by the grace given to me I bid every one among you not to think of himself more highly than he ought to think, but to think with sober judgment" (Rom. 12:3). True humility calls also for honesty in appraising the character of others. Not until one is humble is one ready to become great; but then, being truly humble, he will not be aware of this fact. Humility—and similarly greatness—ceases to exist when it becomes conscious and proud of itself.

Pride, which is the antithesis of humility, lies at the root of the God-complex. Through pride, man is rendered vulnerable. He becomes an easy prey to hurt feelings. The humble man, however, cherishes no illusions concerning himself; he does not feel that it is incumbent upon him to play a role or to maintain an appearance of greatness. He can be himself without fear of exposure.

When a man is filled with pride, he is constantly tormented by the fear of being shown to be inadequate. He must reassure himself repeatedly of his importance and extraordinary worth; he must impress others repeatedly of his superior ability. He fears detection and demotion. The humble man escapes these things. He can willingly accept his humanity with its attendant limitations. He can be happy in the lot which is commensurate with his ability. Defeat does not discourage him unduly, because he realizes that some failures are to be expected. He is not plagued by a perfectionist pattern for his life.

The minister is at his best when he realizes that his life is but an instrument for God to use. He should cease trying to be a dynamo which will generate spiritual power and be content to be a conduit through which God's power will flow. He is at his best when he is being used by a power greater than his own. When he permits God to use him, he will rise to unsuspected heights and become a blessing to all about him.

But this much-to-be-desired humility will not come unless one is willing for it to come. The minister, therefore, must cease striving to maintain the myth of superiority. He must face reality and put his trust in God.

There are some things that can be accomplished only by trying hard; there are other things that can never be accomplished by trying hard. The latter can be accomplished only by *giving up.*

Pulpit power, for example, is experienced only when the minister is a surrendered instrument in God's hands. The confidence which he has in God relaxes him, gives him a sense of freedom. Similarly, peace of mind is achieved by the minister only when he relinquishes all his fretful and vain strivings for self-advancement. Power in prayer is experienced only when the seeker after God's blessing becomes willing that God's will, not his own, shall be done in all things.

We are, in a sense, like vessels appointed for the Lord's use. We need to be filled with spiritual power. But before our lives can be filled, they need to be emptied of what is already there. The emptying precedes the filling, and the filling comes from beyond us and without any effort on our part.

There are ministers who have permitted themselves to become so anxious and tense over their responsibilities that they have not been able to sleep at night. Some have risen from their beds, denying themselves proper rest, to spend the night praying for some wayward man or seeking light and help in connection with some pastoral problem. Such a practice is unnatural, even injurious to one's physical health; what is more, it is likely to prove ineffectual. The minister would do better to pray at a time when prayer is appropriate. He should rest, when night comes, and having committed himself and his work to God, leave the issue in God's hands. God is faithful, but apparently many ministers do not believe this. They work and pray as though everything depended on their own efforts.

It steadies one to remember that God not only calls the stars by name but also knows by name every individual in all earth's teeming millions. God holds us all in the hollow of his hand. This is the word of Jesus. If the minister will accept it, there will be a reflection of it in all that he does and says. His life will take on a new calmness and orderliness.

In many instances it will be well for the minister to fortify his life with a sense of humor.

He may be inclined to take himself much too seriously. Sometimes, in his intensity, every phase of his life seems to be fraught with crisis. Everything that happens is either a major triumph or a major catastrophe. He attaches too much significance to his decisions, actions, and utterances.

The minister with a sense of humor will not take too seriously the mishaps that come to him. He will not be overwhelmed by them. Neither will he be unduly elated by his successes. Above all, he will take himself with a grain of salt. He will be able to laugh at himself and to smile at the foibles of others. He will be cynical toward none; least of all, toward himself.

He will be tolerant whether he looks through a window or into a mirror.

Sir William Osler said: "Lift up one hand to heaven and thank your stars if they have given you the proper sense to enable you to appreciate the inconceivably droll situations in which we catch our fellow creatures." To this statement we are inclined to add: "and in which we catch ourselves."

This seasoning sense of humor is an indispensable ingredient of healthy mindedness. He who possesses it will not permit himself to be maneuvered by his ambitions into a false position, which if once accepted cannot be relinquished without mortification. His sense of humor will reveal to him at once the absurd and ludicrous nature of the position he is tempted to assume.

Of course, humor can be overdone. The minister will do himself harm if he constantly strives to be funny. He has not been called to be a comedian. He had best leave that role to the professional entertainers. If he spends too much time telling funny stories, some of his hearers may conclude that he has not experienced sufficiently the poignancy of life to be sympathetic with them and capable of understanding their needs.

Let the minister pray for the proper religious attitude.
To begin with, he needs to become intellectually honest.
Intellectual honesty involves abhorrence for the lie in the
soul, fully as much as for the lie upon the lips. When there
is no lie in the soul, there will be no false position which
must be maintained at any cost. When there is no false
position which must be maintained, there will be no need
to pretend that one possesses divine, or even markedly superior, attributes.

Sometimes a minister prefers to think of God in Old
Testament, rather than New Testament, terms. He is in-
trigued with the idea of divine wrath, captivated by the
idea of divine judgment. He finds enjoyment in the prospect of the destruction of evildoers. This frame of mind is
then reflected in both his life and his preaching. He moves
in the direction of extermination, rather than regeneration;
his pulpit messages are denunciatory, rather than concilia-
tory. Like an avenging angel, he swoops down upon evil
wherever he finds it. In his attempts to purge his church,
he sets people at odds with one another. He feels that
he knows infallibly who are the wheat and who are the
tares. So long as he is the implement which puts into effect
the divine judgment, what concern is it of his if occasionally
some of the wheat is uprooted along with the tares!

Pugnacity is not one of the characteristics of the true
Christian temper. Certainly it is no mark of divine ap-
proval, if the minister, everywhere he goes, sets the saints
to fighting among themselves.

The characteristic and predominant Christian trait is
love. When we behold love, we know that God is present;
for love is of God. He who loves not, knows not God;
he has not been born of God, for God is love.

It is feared that all too often a minister thinks of this fact only when he is seeking a text for a sermon. He does not think of it as referring to himself and his relationship to his congregation. Let the minister pray for grace to love his flock, with all their imperfections and immaturities. This, rather than denunciation, is his divinely appointed responsibility. To be sure, he will encounter opposition. This is to be expected, for he is the representative of a holier way of living. But the opposition he meets is to be overcome, not by censure, but by patient love.

Let the pastor pray for grace to *grow* in love, realizing that every obedience to the impulse of love will make him a better leader and a holier man. The soul so prompted can be trusted.

Let the minister cultivate also the spirit of gratitude.

Accepting kindnesses as one's due, rather than showing gratitude for them, is one of the most irritating manifestations of the God-complex. The God-complex is the ultimate in self-centeredness, and it shows itself in the offhand way in which a minister affected with it treats other persons.

A layman has related the disillusioning experience he had with two clergymen whom he entertained in his home, while they were on an assignment which took them across the country.

"Knowing that their expense account was limited, and believing that they were traveling in a good cause, I arranged accommodations for them. I took them out to lunch twice and they had two meals in my home. My wife gave up her plans for those afternoons to prepare meals for them. I spent ten dollars in cash and twenty-four working hours with them. However, our guests spoke no word of comment or appreciation when the meals were finished."

Then this layman, perplexed and irritated by what appeared to him to have been thoughtless and ungrateful behavior, related a somewhat similar experience he had with two chaplains. This man and his wife graciously invited these chaplains into their home and gave them a home-cooked dinner.

"We thought we were doing them a kindness," he explained, "but it seems that in accepting our invitation they thought they were doing *us* a favor, merely by presenting their holy selves at our table. We expected a quiet, after-dinner visit in the living room, but it did not take place. There was a wrestling match at camp that night which they did not think they could miss."

Granted that these were exceptional incidents, and granted also that in both instances the omission of words of gratitude undoubtedly was thoughtless, still the incidents suggest too much self-concern, too little regard for the feelings of others.

Let the minister beware of thinking of himself as being of so exalted a status that the consideration shown him by others can be accepted as a phase of *noblesse oblige*. Let him beware when he begins to take courtesies for granted, and fails to express sincere thanks for the many kindnesses which people show him out of the goodness of their hearts.

Let him learn to think of people, and what he can do for them, instead of thinking of himself, and what they can do for him.

If he would join the ranks of humanity, let him cultivate the grace of gratitude. This grace will make him one among his fellows. That is where he must be, if he is to serve them. And that is what he must do, if he is to fulfill his ministry.

7

COMING TO TERMS WITH REALITY

UNQUESTIONABLY, THE MINISTER, even as every other person, must come to terms with reality. This is a real world in which he finds himself, and the conditions under which he must live are hard and uncompromising. In his life he encounters much that is strange, sometimes much that is hostile. Furthermore, he realizes that his stay in the world is limited. His life is overshadowed constantly by the inevitability of death. Life and death are realities from which there is no escape. To protest against these realities is of no avail. To surrender to hopeless rage and to beat upon the bars of this earthly prison will accomplish nothing.

The Adjustment to Life

Man may not run away from life, if he would achieve any degree of self-realization. Neither may he ignore life, if he would attain any measure of maturity.

In taking account of life, man must come to grips with it as it actually is, not as he could wish it to be. If there were perfection in the world, no room would be left for growth and improvement. It has been said that growth is the surest evidence of life. The struggle to grow gives meaning to existence. The imperfections which man sees within himself and within his surroundings constitute his challenge.

While acknowledging that there will always be imperfections in life, man should not permit himself to be content with them. Neither growth nor achievement is possible where there is complete contentment, whether it be with oneself or with one's environment. Complacency stultifies and deadens. The complacent individual vegetates, rather than lives.

There is, therefore, a dissatisfaction apart from which man will never live positively and constructively. Those who have left their mark upon the world for good have felt a "divine discontent." They have not been willing to accept the status quo. Instead, they have been the crusaders, the builders of a new and nobler order. They have kept themselves free from cynicism, fatalism, and despair, and have labored constantly to make the world better.

Man must recognize the fact that there is suffering in the world, and he must accept his share of the anguish without surrendering himself either to hate or to fear. It is natural but somewhat profitless to ask, "Why must people suffer?" Sometimes there is a direct connection between a person's sufferings and his mistakes and misdeeds. Sometimes the connection is indirect or remote. At other times, there seems to be no connection whatever. In many instances the suffering seems to come, without rhyme or reason, upon the innocent. One must simply accept the fact that all people, in the course of their lives, experience suffering in some form or other.

The acceptance of suffering, however, need not be a merely passive attitude. The wise man learns to respond to suffering constructively, as did Florence Nightingale, Clara Barton, and Dr. Albert Schweitzer. They were moved by the suffering which they saw to efforts to alleviate it.

Whether the suffering is one's own or another's, one must endeavor to turn it to some good account. One must let the endurance of it be a means of character growth.

No two persons are exactly alike in appearance or in thought. Consequently, when a man surveys the human scene, he is certain to find many persons who do not agree with him. In their conduct they do not conform to his ideas as to what is right. Some will persistently disappoint him, even oppose him. There is, then, an important adjustment to one's fellow men which needs to be made. One must love one's neighbor and endeavor to help him, and one must do this without attempting to dominate him and without demanding of him exact conformity to one's own ideas.

Man must expect some frustrating experiences. To be able to accept them without losing heart and to persevere in good works is a mark of maturity. Whereas a child wants immediate results, the mature person can "run with patience." Some problems can be solved only by self-denial and persistent effort. He must learn "to labor and to wait." Through such living has come all that has been of lasting benefit to mankind.

Man needs to accept the fact that in his deepest being he is alone. Although he lives in a society, there is that within him which no one else can fully comprehend or share. In a very real sense, "Each man will have to bear his own load" (Gal. 6:5). There is, then, this loneliness which lies in the depths of every life, and each man needs to learn to contemplate it without fear.

Thus, although in the midst of a world which he is prone to think of as commonplace, every man stands in the presence of a great mystery—his own being. Within

his soul—and this is all-important—he can have fellowship with God. "The kingdom of God is within you"
(Luke 17:21, margin). God can be the believer's supreme
delight, the source and measure of his integrity and true
self-respect.

Strengthened by the sense of his sincerity and by the
assurance that he can depend upon God for help, he will
not falter when the winds of human opinion blow against
him; he will not despair however severe the storms of human rejection which break upon him.

The Adjustment to Death

Even as man must adjust himself to life, so he must
adjust himself to death. In his mortal span, the elements
of life and death are inextricably mingled. It seems that
almost as soon as he is born he begins to die. Because
death is inevitable, he must reconcile himself to the coming of it. He must learn to look death steadily in the face.
He must be able to embrace death without a spirit of
fatalism, fear, or regret. And he must be prepared to do
this, whatever the hour of its coming may be.

Now, in order to accept the fact of death, it is not necessary to despise life. Life should not be called evil in order
that death may be called good. Neither should the future
life be depreciated in order that this life may be counted
good. Some have asserted that it is enough to live one life
at a time. However, if we analyze the situation correctly,
we must affirm that man is at his best when he lives his
earthly life against the backdrop of eternity. His spirit
must transcend time, place, and things. In a true and profound sense, his life must be infused with a sense of the
eternal. This eternal reference, this deep quality of life,

is known as it should be known only in the full glory of Christ. "This is eternal life, that they know thee the only true God, and Jesus Christ whom thou hast sent" (John 17:3).

Life is lived best when one has come to terms with death through faith in Christ, in whom is "the power of an indestructible life" (Heb. 7:16). In some quarters it has been popular to belittle this hope of eternal life. However, when man has discounted it, he has found his stay on earth increasingly futile. It is possible that much of our modern unhappiness and frustration has arisen for just this reason. Man lives with a "lift," only if he knows that there is that within him which through Jesus Christ will never die.

If a man is to adjust himself satisfactorily to the certainty of death, he must beware of setting his heart too firmly on this mortal life and its impedimenta. He must not fix his affections upon the world, nor upon the things which are in the world. He must not become entangled with the affairs of this life. True, he must have a certain attachment to this life. He has a work to do and a place to fill. He must serve his day. He must grasp the hand of his fellow man with the warmth of love. But he must clearly understand that this world passes away.

He must, therefore, recognize the brevity of his stay here. He must know that his days are swifter than a weaver's shuttle and as quick to fade as the beauty of a summer flower. But despite the brevity of his existence, he must live without haste, desperation, or frenzy. Perhaps he vaguely feels that by living in haste he can prolong his days or overcome his mortality, but by so doing, he succeeds only in abbreviating his life and adding to its burden and sorrow. Man must learn to walk with measured tread. He must learn to work with a certain deliberation. Otherwise, he will not escape the damaging effects of haste.

Man, repeatedly, is called upon to stand beside an open grave. If the pangs of his sorrow permit him to think clearly, his soul responds to the assertions of the seers and prophets from time beyond memory that man is more than dust, that death is not man's destiny. Indeed, he feels within himself a kinship with that which is invisible and eternal in the universe. Heaven has lain around him too long to be unreal. He trusts in immortality.

This great hope has inspired man's noblest language and most elevated thoughts. It has prompted sacrificial living and triumphant dying. The Christian looks upon the empty tomb. His heart thrills to the Easter message. He worships the risen Savior. He hears the sublime words: "I am the resurrection and the life; he who believes in me, though he die, yet shall he live, and whoever lives and believes in me shall never die" (John 11:25).

It is not given to man to know in specific terms what lies beyond the grave. That realm is too vast, too mysterious, for mortal mind to fathom it. He can know it only with that intuitive knowledge which his soul possesses and which will not be denied. But it is enough for him to have in mind that which has been written: "Eye hath not seen, nor ear heard, neither have entered into the heart of man, the things which God hath prepared for them that love him" (1 Cor. 2:9, KJV).

William James, in his monumental work *The Varieties of Religious Experience,* makes this statement: "The further limits of our being plunge, it seems to me, into an altogether other dimension of existence from the sensible and merely 'understandable' world. Name it the mystical region, or the supernatural region, whichever you choose. . . . We belong to it in a more intimate sense than that in which we belong to the visible world, for we belong in the most intimate sense wherever our ideals belong. Yet the unseen region in question is not merely ideal, for it produces effects in this world. When we commune with it, work is actually done upon our finite personality, for we are turned into new men, and consequences in the way of conduct follow in the natural world upon our regenerative change. But that which produces effects within another reality must be termed a reality itself. . . . The total expression of human experience, as I view it objectively, invincibly urges me beyond the narrow 'scientific' bounds. Assuredly, the real world is of a different temperament—more intricately built than physical science allows."[1]

Something within man cries out for the assurance that his life has meaning, that he does not walk and work alone. He is in bondage to this dependence, although he sometimes protests that he is not. Being proud, he may not wish to admit his inadequacy, but it matters much to him whether he is working alone or has someone working with him. Something within him imperatively demands ultimate reality, worth that transcends all human efforts, and that lends meaning to this transient life. Man can live more bravely, can serve more faithfully, and come to the end of his days with finer resignation, if he believes there is permanent value in his struggle for the better life, and if he perceives that there is an upward slope, as well as poignancy, to human existence.

[1] From *The Varieties of Religious Experience,* by William James. Copyright, 1902, by William James. Longmans, Green and Company.

Man, of course, should look beyond his mortality. Because he has not done so, generation after generation has been burdened with a sense of depravity and impending doom. There are those who have preached the imminent end of all things, but surprisingly the anticipated denouement has not come. Many times the curve of moral living has dropped very low and man's pessimism respecting himself has seemed justified; but God has not cast off man. Instead, God is still working out his plan. Out of suffering has come growth; out of death, life.

In the providence of God, mankind has a destiny and he will meet that destiny someday. Throughout the pages of Holy Writ runs a heavenly harmony, and no earthly clamor can silence it. Similarly, the thought of God has been like soft music in man's soul. Through the procession of the centuries, the melody has persisted. God has been working his purposes out, and man has been given a part in them. The whole creation has been groaning in travail together (Rom. 8:22) while awaiting this consummation, this coming of the kingdom of God, this rule of God over the nations and over the hearts of men. There is a rightness in the universe that will not be denied.

Every human life is a part of this whole. Nothing that is offered to God is ever lost. Every word and every deed of every good man who has ever lived is a part of this grand design. The man of God is neither a puppet nor a futile actor in the drama of life. He is God's man. Within the framework of his human limitations, he can co-operate with the Eternal God.

DATE DUE

BW· 1601